CW00557805

Cassino 1944

Breaking the Gustav Line

Campaign • 134

Cassino 1944

Breaking the Gustav Line

Ken Ford · Illustrated by Howard Gerrard

Series editor Lee Johnson

First published in Great Britain in 2004 by Osprey Publishing,
Midland House, West Way, Botley, Oxford OX2 0PH, UK
443 Park Avenue South, New York, NY 10016, USA
Email: info@ospreypublishing.com

© 2004 Osprey Publishing Ltd.

All rights reserved. Apart from any fair dealing for the purpose of private study,
research, criticism or review, as permitted under the Copyright, Designs and
Patents Act, 1988, no part of this publication may be reproduced, stored in a
retrieval system, or transmitted in any form or by any means, electronic,
electrical, chemical, mechanical, optical, photocopying, recording or otherwise,
without the prior written permission of the copyright owner. Enquiries should be
addressed to the Publishers.

A CIP catalogue record for this book is available from the British Library

ISBN 978-1-84176-623-2

Editor: Lee Johnson
Design: The Black Spot
Index by David Worthington
Maps by The Maps Studio
3D bird's-eye views by The Black Spot
Battlescene artwork by Howard Gerrard
Originated by PPS Grasmere Ltd, Leeds, UK
Printed in China through World Print Ltd.
Typeset in Helvetica Neue and ITC New Baskerville

08 09 10 11 12 14 13 12 11 10 9 8 7 6 5

For a catalogue of all books published by Osprey Military
and Aviation please contact:

NORTH AMERICA
Osprey Direct, C/o Random House Distribution Center,
400 Hahn Road, Westminster, MD 21157, USA
E-mail: info@ospreydirect.com

ALL OTHER REGIONS
Osprey Direct UK, P.O. Box 140, Wellingborough,
Northants, NN8 2FA, UK
E-mail: info@ospreydirect.co.uk

www.ospreypublishing.com

Author's note

The Orders of Battle in this volume are a 'snapshot' of
those units that fought on the Cassino front and at Anzio.
Many divisions were switched between sectors and fought
on both fronts in different corps and armies. Some,
especially German units, were split up and rarely fought
with their parent organisation. Only the major organisations
are shown, many smaller ad hoc units were raised at
various times, again especially by the Germans, to provide
a tactical reserve or to plug a gap in the line.

Artist's note

Readers may care to note that the original paintings from
which the colour plates in this book were prepared are
available for private sale. All reproduction copyright
whatsoever is retained by the Publishers. All enquiries
should be addressed to:

Howard Gerrard
11 Oaks Road,
Tenterden,
Kent
TN30 6RD
UK

The Publishers regret that they can enter into no
correspondence upon this matter.

KEY TO MILITARY SYMBOLS

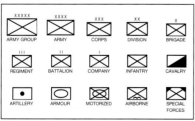

CONTENTS

ADVANCE TO THE GUSTAV LINE

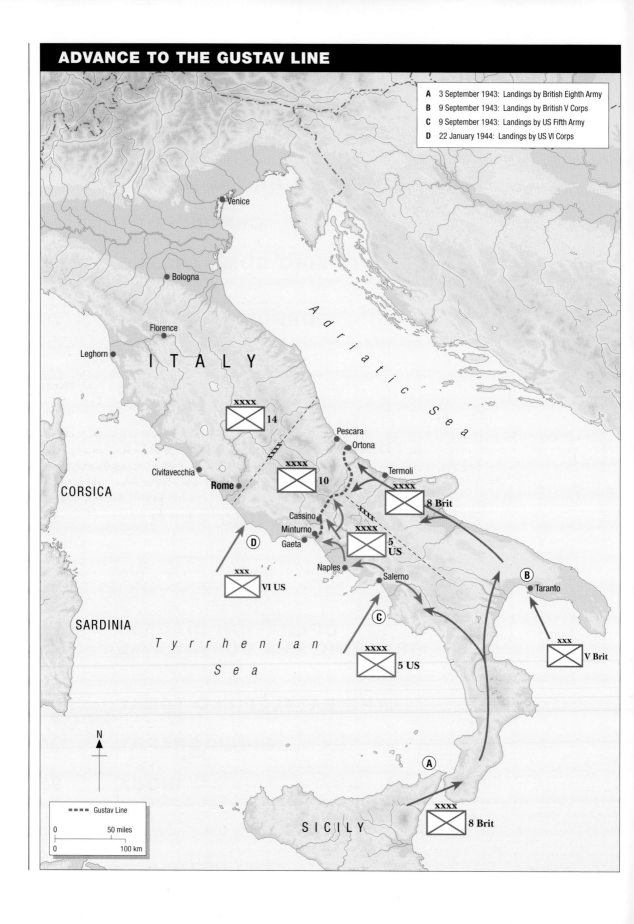

A 3 September 1943: Landings by British Eighth Army
B 9 September 1943: Landings by British V Corps
C 9 September 1943: Landings by US Fifth Army
D 22 January 1944: Landings by US VI Corps

Venice

Bologna

Florence

Leghorn

I T A L Y

Adriatic Sea

XXXX
14

Pescara
Ortona

Termoli

Civitavecchia

XXXX
10

Rome

XXXX
8 Brit

CORSICA

Cassino
Minturno
Gaeta

XXXX
5 US

D

XXX
VI US

Naples

Salerno

B

Taranto

SARDINIA

T y r r h e n i a n

S e a

XXXX
5 US

C

XXX
V Brit

N

Gustav Line

0   50 miles

0   100 km

A

S I C I L Y

XXXX
8 Brit

ORIGINS OF THE BATTLE

The final defeat and capitulation of Axis forces in North Africa in May 1943, whilst a significant military success, left the Allies with the problem of where to strike next. The most obvious move was to follow the retreating enemy across the Mediterranean Sea and open a front in Sicily and Italy, taking the fight into the Fascist alliance's own backyard. This strategy had much to commend it and was the preferred choice of Britain's Prime Minister, Winston Churchill. He felt that such an attack would lead rapidly to the collapse of Mussolini's fascist regime in Italy. It would also draw in and tie down German forces that could otherwise be committed elsewhere, in particular against the Russians. The Americans thought differently. They were suspicious of Churchill's motives in the Mediterranean and were against any operations that might distract from or weaken the cross-Channel invasion planned for the spring of 1944.

Churchill felt that the Allies could not just sit and wait for the invasion of France to take place, they had to maintain the pressure on the Axis forces. An invasion of Italy would at least give the British and Americans a lodgement on the mainland of Europe that, if successful, could provide a route into the occupied territories. It was finally agreed, therefore, that an attack would be launched against Sicily in July, followed by the invasion of Italy immediately after the island had been captured.

An American soldier stands in the ruins of Cassino and views the battlefield at the end of the struggle to take Montecassino. Every square metre of the town, mountain and countryside had been pounded to rubble and crater by bomb, shot and shell. (US National Archives)

7

The landings in Sicily began on 10 July 1943 and it took almost two months of savage fighting before all enemy resistance was eliminated. On 3 September, Montgomery's British Eighth Army crossed over the narrow Straits of Messina and landed on the toe of Italy. Mussolini's government fell almost immediately and on 8 September a new Italian administration, headed by Marshal Badoglio, announced Italy's surrender. The next day US Fifth Army landed at Salerno, south of Naples, and British V Corps came ashore at Taranto.

The collapse of Mussolini's fascist state did not, however, bring an end to hostilities in Italy. Hitler moved quickly, ordering his forces to take control of the country, seizing all important strategic installations and disarming and disbanding apathetic Italian troops. New German divisions were immediately moved across the border and the country was swiftly brought under the heel of the Third Reich. The speed of the German take-over took the Allies by surprise and the ferocity with which the landings at Salerno were resisted gave them great cause for concern. It soon became clear that the fighting in Italy would be just as complex and intense as the previous struggles in North Africa. Hitler had ordered that no territory be given up without a fight.

Once committed to the Italian campaign, the Allies found themselves struggling to overcome not only the enemy, but the terrain as well. Much of Italy is ideally suited for defensive warfare. The Appenine mountain range is the spine of Italy, virtually splitting the peninsula in two. On either side of these mountains are narrow coastal plains, leaving little room to deploy large armies. With the Allies landing in the south, the advance northwards would be confined to these small coastal strips. As they advanced north the Allies would be confronted by a series of rivers that flowed down from the Appenines, cutting across the peninsula. They were flanked by spurs of high ground from the mountains themselves, and each

US troops and tanks moving up to the front line in Italy. The bad winter weather forced the Allies to make good use of the few metalled roads available to move their armour. (Imperial War Museum, TAP13491)

A group of British 6-pdr anti-tank guns under camouflage during one of the earlier battles in Italy. The guns are mounted on American T-48 half-track gun carriages. (US National Archives)

formed a natural defence line that the Germans were all too capable of exploiting. No sooner had the Allies overcome one defensive line and resumed their advance than they would discover another barring their way. So formidable are the obstacles to waging war effectively in the Italian peninsula that military strategists have on several occasions classified it as 'technically absurd'.

When the American Fifth Army landed at Salerno, Generalfeldmarschall Kesselring, Commander-in-Chief South, had only a few divisions of German Tenth Army under his direct control with which to counter them. The bulk of the German forces in Italy was still north of Rome under the command of Generalfeldmarschall Erwin Rommel, Commander-in-Chief North, and were engaged in disarming the Italian Army. Kesselring's forces were able to put up such stiff resistance, however, that the Allied landings tottered on the brink of failure. This stubborn defence by Generaloberst von Vietinghoff and his German Tenth Army against both the Americans and the British led Hitler to believe that Italy could be defended, or that his forces could at least exact a high price from the Allies for its conquest.

Hitler was impressed with Kesselring's handling of the Allied attacks and with Tenth Army's dogged defence. He was less pleased by Rommel's advice to withdraw all forces behind Rome and construct a defensive line through the mountains in the north of Italy. He decided to disregard Rommel's advice and reinforce Kesselring. He also gave Kesselring the responsibility of defending the whole country as Commander Army Group 'C'. Hitler directed that nothing to the south of Rome was to be given up without a struggle. Rommel was posted to France to oversee the construction of the Atlantic Wall and to take charge of the measures required to repel any Allied invasion along the Channel coast.

During the autumn of 1943, US Fifth Army advanced northwards from its Salerno beachhead along the western coastal strip; British Eighth Army drove up the east coast alongside the Adriatic Sea. Both advances were slow and dogged. The Germans made excellent use of the river barriers blocking the way. In the east, Montgomery faced the Biferno, the Trigno and the Sangro rivers. In the west, Mark Clark was confronted by the Volturno and the Garigliano. Two of these rivers, one in the east and one in the west – the Sangro and Garigliano – almost meet at their head-waters, virtually bisecting the country at its narrowest point. Kesselring decided to use these rivers as the anchor of a strong defensive line across Italy. This fortified barrier, named the Gustav Line, was to be heavily defended with concrete emplacements, mines, wire and resistance posts. To give his engineers time to complete the defences, Kesselring planned a series of spoiling actions along lesser defence lines further south to delay the Allied advance. The first of these was south of Naples, the next along the Volturno and Biferno rivers. As the Allies pushed north and the weather turned cold, they encountered the Winter Lines around Monte Massico and the River Trigno, and finally, as an outpost of the Gustav Line, a lesser defensive line called the Bernhard Line was built just short of the River Garigliano.

It took three months for both Allied armies to fight their way up to the Gustav Line. Clark's Fifth Army saw the heaviest of the fighting on the western side. Kesselring deduced that the route taken by Montgomery's Eighth Army along the Adriatic coast was less attractive to the Allies. The succession of rivers and coastal mountain barriers rendered it unsuitable for any kind of mobile warfare. It was difficult to use large formations effectively on the narrow coastal strip and armour could only be deployed in 'penny packets' in the support of infantry. The Germans realised that the main thrust towards Rome would have to come in the west. The ground there was somewhat better than on the eastern side of the Appenines and transport vehicles and armour could operate on two of the roads in significant numbers. Route 7 followed a path along the coastal strip between the sea and the Aurunci Mountains and Route 6 ran through the Liri valley. Kesselring decided to build his strongest defences in this sector.

The Monastery on top of Montecassino before the Allied bombing, seen from the valley in front of Snakeshead Ridge. (Imperial War Museum, MH11250)

By December 1943 the Allies had reached the Gustav Line, but frontline units were in need of rest and replenishment. Three months of continual fighting had reduced their fighting strength and depleted their resources. They had also endured the onset of the Italian winter. Heavy rain had reduced roads, tracks and forward areas to seas of glutinous mud. Much of the fighting had been in the mountains and the lack of metalled roads had meant most supplies had to be transported by porters or mule trains. In the 20th Century's first truly mechanised war, the combatants found themselves operating with methods that were practically medieval. From the military point of view, it may have made sense for the Allies to pause, regroup and plan for a spring offensive. The need to maintain pressure on the German forces to prevent them being withdrawn to other fronts made this politically unacceptable. This opening of a second front in Europe had brought some relief to the Red Army and the pressure had to be maintained on Kesselring's troops at all cost.

Montgomery attacked across the River Sangro in strength at the end of November 1943 and breached the defence line. He advanced 14 miles during the next four weeks and his 1st Canadian Division fought its way to the outskirts of Ortona. Here the offensive stalled, beaten by the strength of German resistance, the difficult terrain and the onset of bad weather. Any significant advance by British Eighth Army along this route was clearly out of the question until the spring. It was now up to LtGen Mark Clark's US Fifth Army in the west to continue the struggle and break the Gustav Line.

CHRONOLOGY

Castle Hill (Point 193) seen from the town. Extensive rebuilding work is restoring the medieval building to its former glory. This side of Castle Hill was out of sight of the enemy on Monastery Hill and provided the only route up to the ruined castle. Every item of food, water and ammunition had to be manhandled up this near vertical face to resupply the position. (Ken Ford)

1943

12 May General Jürgen von Arnim surrenders all Axis forces in North Africa.

10 July British and American forces under the command of General Dwight D. Eisenhower invade Sicily.

17 August Allies enter Messina and all German resistance ends in Sicily, but over 60,000 Germans have escaped to safety on the Italian mainland.

3 September British Eighth Army crosses the narrow straits of Messina and creates a lodgement on the toe of Italy. Four years after the outbreak of war, British troops are back on the mainland of Europe.

8 September Italy makes public its surrender to the Allies.

9 September LtGen Mark Clark lands his US Fifth Army at Salerno.

6 October Naples is captured by US Fifth Army.

14 October Americans attack across the River Volturno.

22 October Montgomery's Eighth Army force a crossing of the River Trigno and his troops continue to drive up the Adriatic coast of Italy

15 November Alexander halts his forces so that they might regroup ready for an attack against the German Winter Line defences.

24 November British Eighth Army cross the River Sangro and enter the defences of the Winter Line, but are halted when they reach Ortona the following month.

3 December US Fifth Army fights its way into the defences of the German Winter Line and begins a month long struggle through the mountains.

1944

12 January American troops arrive on the River Garigliano and plan their attack against the Gustav Line. The main axis of their advance will be up the Liri valley and breaking into this valley will preoccupy Allied forces for the next four months. The French Expeditionary Corps moves into the mountains north of Cassino and makes contact with the defences of the Gustav Line. After four days of fighting, General Juin's corps is forced to a halt.

RIGHT **American troops resort to brute force to extricate a jeep from thick mud. The winter rains and atrocious weather during the Gustav Line campaign rendered open ground impassable to wheeled traffic. (US National Archives)**

ABOVE **American signalmen repair another break in the line. The unreliability of radio sets and the possibility of the interception of orders by the enemy, led to great reliance on telephonic messaging to keep forward positions in touch with command in the rear. Unfortunately, it took just one tracked vehicle passing over the exposed cables to sever all communications. (US National Archives)**

17 January US Fifth Army begins its assault on the Gustav Line with British X Corps attacking across the River Garigliano and the French trying once more to break into the German fortifications. After days of fighting, in which some gains are made, both attacks grind to a halt in the face of severe enemy resistance.

20 January US 36th 'Texas' Division attacks across the Rapido in an attempt to break into the Liri valley, but is forced back after two days of fighting.

22 January Major General John P. Lucas lands his US VI Corps at Anzio near Rome in an attempt to outflank the Gustav Line. GFM Kesselring reacts with admirable speed and moves General Eberhard von Mackensen's Fourteenth Army against the landings to seal the perimeter before Lucas is able to make a move inland.

24 January US II Corps uses its 34th Division to try to get across the Rapido north of the town of Cassino, behind the defences around Montecassino, and into the Liri valley. The attack has some initial success when American troops move onto the high ground to the rear of Cassino, however, they are halted on the hills close to Monastery Hill.

30 January Gen Lucas begins his breakout battle at Anzio. Superior German forces resist his moves and the attack fails after days of heavy fighting.

An aerial view of the Cassino position. Snakeshead Ridge is the line of hills immediately above the Monastery in the picture. The village of Cairo is on the far right and the entrance into Liri valley and the road to Rome is on the left. (US National Archives)

15 February General Bernard C. Freyberg and his New Zealand II Corps are given the task of capturing Cassino and Montecassino. The battle begins with the complete destruction of the Monastery by heavy bombers. 4th Indian Division and 2nd New Zealand Division attack the town and the Monastery without success. The Maori Battalion captures Cassino's Railway Station but is forced out by a German counterattack, while the 7th Indian Brigade fails to even capture its start line.

16 February Von Mackensen launches his major offensive against the landings at Anzio. Despite forcing US VI Corps back almost to its final stop line, he is unable to break the American resistance. Kesselring calls off the counterattack on 19 February and German policy towards Anzio settles down to one of containment.

15 March Gen Freyberg launches the third battle for Cassino. The attack starts this time with the complete destruction of the town by Allied bombers. Freyberg then attacks down the Rapido into the town, but even after eight days of fighting is still unable to evict the German 1st Parachute Division from the ruins. On the flanks of Montecassino, 4th Indian Division occupy the Castle and the Gurkhas seize Hangman's Hill just under the walls of the Monastery, but are finally forced to retreat after nine days of fighting. An unsuccessful armoured attack is launched against the rear of the Abbey along Cavendish Road built by the engineers from the village of Cairo. Tanks reach the important strongpoint at Albaneta Farm, only to have the attack stall when most of the armour is destroyed.

23 March–10 May Preparations are made for a major offensive against the Gustav Line. Alexander shifts his army boundaries and brings over the bulk of British Eighth Army from the Adriatic front. He plans a new attack with all the units he is able to bring into the line. Codenamed Operation Diadem, this offensive will put four corps into the attack simultaneously. The main drive will be by British XIII corps up the Liri valley where it will join with US VI Corps who will break out of the Anzio lodgement and advance eastwards to cut off the retreating German Tenth Army.

11 May–20 May Operation Diadem begins. US II Corps attacks from its Garigliano bridgehead and advances up Route 7. The French Expeditionary Corps attacks through the Aurunci Mountains and then swings down into the Liri valley. British XIII Corps cross the Rapido, break through the Gustav Line and sweep up towards the new defensive line called the Hitler Line. Polish II Corps attack Monastery Hill but are beaten back. They try again on **17 May** and successfully occupy the Monastery two days later.

23 May French, Canadian and British troops attack the Hitler Line. US VI Corps begins its breakout battle at Anzio.

25 May The Hitler Line begins to fail and the enemy start to withdraw towards Rome. US VI Corps attack through the perimeter around Anzio and link up with US II Corps coming up from the south.

26 May Gen Mark Clark gives new orders to his Fifth Army and decides to head for Rome to liberate the city. The original plan to trap the retreating German Tenth Army is given a lesser priority, allowing the bulk of von Vietinghoff's forces to escape.

4 June Rome is liberated, but the battle for Italy goes on for the next 11 months.

Cassino town, its castle and the Monastery before any of them were subjected to bombing or shell fire. The picture clearly shows how the castle dominated the town and the Monastery dominated everything. (US National Archives)

OPPOSING COMMANDERS

Gen Sir Henry Maitland Wilson, Supreme Allied Commander Mediterranean (right), talks with his American deputy, LtGen Jacob Devers. (Imperial War Museum, NA 10848)

The Allied command structure in the Mediterranean saw great changes at the end of 1943. These were largely a result of the increased tempo of planning for the Allied landings in France – Operation Overlord. Most significant was the departure of General Dwight D. Eisenhower, the Supreme Commander. He left the theatre to take up his post as Allied Supreme Commander for the D-Day landings. General Sir Bernard Law Montgomery also left for England to take command of the land forces for the invasion of France. Replacing these two men were soldiers of great fighting ability and long experience in the Middle East. General Sir Henry Maitland Wilson became Supreme Allied Commander Mediterranean and Lieutenant-General Sir Oliver Leese took over the command of British Eighth Army.

There was no disruption or loss of cohesion in the Allied command as a result of this reshuffle, as two of the major players remained *in situ*. General Sir Harold Alexander continued as Commander Fifteenth Army Group and Lieutenant General Mark Clark remained Commander of US Fifth Army.

The changes made by Hitler in November had simplified the German command situation in Italy. The removal of Rommel from the theatre left Generalfeldmarschall Kesselring as C-in-C Italy with a direct line to Hitler and the Oberkommando Wehrmacht (OKW) – supreme HQ of the German armed forces. It also gave him more of a free rein to implement his defensive strategy for Italy.

ALLIED COMMANDERS

The appointment of **General Sir Henry Maitland Wilson** to head the Allied effort in the Mediterranean theatre was made with diplomatic as well as military considerations. Wilson was a veteran of many campaigns with a good deal of active service experience. He was a veteran of both the Boer War and World War I. At the outbreak of World War II he headed the British Army of the Nile. He took part in all of the early battles in North Africa and later served in command of the campaigns in Greece, Iraq and Syria. He was C-in-C Persia-Iraq and Commander British 9th Army before succeeding General Alexander in February 1943 as C-in-C Middle East. He replaced Eisenhower as Supreme Commander Mediterranean on 8 January 1944.

A year earlier, the Chief of the Imperial General Staff, Field Marshal Alanbrooke, had considered Wilson too old and tired for continued high command, but was pleased to reconsider when he realised that the unique talents of the old war-horse could be put to good use in the Mediterranean. With the departure of Eisenhower from the theatre, the Allies needed a commander with good diplomatic skills and administrative ability to maintain relations between British and American forces, rather than a battlefield commander to implement tactics and leadership. Wilson was content to leave the direction of the war in Italy to Alexander, whilst he helped implement the strategy and policies of the politicians.

Subordinate to Gen Wilson was **General Sir Harold Alexander**, Commander Fifteenth Army Group. Alexander was born the third son of the Earl of Caledon and was educated at Harrow. He graduated from Sandhurst in 1911 and gained a commission in the Irish Guards. In the First War he served as a battalion commander and acting brigadier of 4th Guards Brigade, during which time he was wounded twice and won both the MC and DSO. Between the wars he saw service in a variety of staff posts and on India's North West Frontier. In 1937, at the age of 45, he was promoted major-general, at the time the British Army's youngest general. He commanded British 1st Division in France in 1940 and then I Corps in the evacuation at Dunkirk. Alexander was sent to Burma to try to restore the critical situation following the Japanese invasion, but arrived to late to save Rangoon. He soon decided that the whole of Burma would have to be given up and withdrew his forces into India. In August 1942 he took over Near East Command, which later became 18th Army Group (First and Eighth Armies). He was Montgomery's boss in North Africa and continued in that post through the Sicily campaign and the invasion of Italy, although by then his command was designated 15th Army Group (American Fifth Army and British Eighth Army).

Alexander was one of the few senior British generals that the Americans liked. He was not seen as a commander of great strategic ability, but he was a commander who could bring together the fractious collection of Allied generals who served in the Italian theatre. There were many headstrong and difficult generals, as well as politicians, who all had their own ideas on the way the war in Italy should be prosecuted. Alexander had the ability to listen to them all, whatever their nationality, to invite suggestions and to formulate strategy that channelled their energies away from clashes of ego or national pride and into defeating the common enemy.

Commanding British Eighth Army after the departure of Gen Montgomery was **Lieutenant-General Sir Oliver Leese.** He was a veteran of the North African campaign who took over the command with Monty's full blessing. Leese had been commissioned in the Coldstream Guards at the start of the First World War and fought on the Western Front where he was wounded twice and won the DSO. Between the wars he commanded a battalion of his regiment and spent some time as an instructor at the Quetta staff college in India, specialising in tank warfare. In 1940 he was on Lord Gort's staff in France. In 1941 he took command of the Guards Division and converted it to an armoured role. In August 1942, Montgomery summoned him to Egypt to take over XXX Corps, which he then led from El Alamein to Tunis. He took part in the Sicily campaign and in the early battles in Italy as a corps commander. According to a signal he sent to Alanbrooke, Montgomery considered Leese 'the best soldier out here'.

Leese had a very easy-going nature and ran his command on rather informal lines. A humorous man, he was always pictured laughing or smiling. His relaxed style of generalship allowed him to handle the soldiers from many nations that made up his Eighth Army, consisting as

Gen Sir Harold Alexander, Commander Allied Fifteenth Army Group. Alexander had seen action in the First War with the Irish Guards and served in all the major theatres of the Second World War, bar North-West Europe. He had a fine combat record and was well respected by most of his contemporaries. His diplomatic ability enabled him to work effectively with his subordinates from a variety of nationalities. (Ken Ford)

LtGen Mark Wayne Clark, Commander US Fifth Army. Clark became the US Army's youngest three star general when he was promoted to lieutenant general in November 1942. He took command of Fifth Army in December. (US National Archives)

LtGen Alphonse Juin, Commander French Expeditionary Corps (left), in jovial discussion with LtGen Sir Oliver Leese, Commander British Eighth Army (centre) and Gen Sir Harold Alexander Commander Allied Fifteenth Army Group (right). (Imperial War Museum, NA13509)

LtGen Bernard Freyberg VC, Commander New Zealand II Corps, was a true New Zealand hero. During World War I, Freyberg won the Victoria Cross whilst in command of a battalion, was awarded the DSO with two bars, was mentioned in dispatches five times, was wounded on six separate occasions (suffering ten individual wounds) and ended the war as a brigadier-general. (Imperial War Museum, NA10630)

it did of troops from Britain, Canada, India, Poland, Italy and South Africa. Leese was a fighting general who had known only success as a commander. His unpretentious style concealed an individual of great tactical ability.

The second of Alexander's army commanders was **Lieutenant General Mark Clark** who led US Fifth Army. Mark Clark graduated from West Point in 1917 and served on the Western Front during World War I. He was seriously wounded soon after entering combat as a company commander. Between the wars he served on a number of staff appointments and came to the attention of many senior American officers. His promotion was fairly rapid and in April 1942, a few months after America entered the war, Clark became a major general. He served with Eisenhower in the UK helping to organise the build-up of US forces prior to the invasion of North Africa and was appointed Eisenhower's deputy for the 'Torch' landings. His role in the campaign took on a diplomatic element when Clark was given the task of dealing with the various French factions. In November 1942 Clark earned his third star, becoming the youngest lieutenant general in the US Army at the age of 46.

LtGen Mark Clark took command of US Fifth Army in December 1942, but it was not until the invasion of Italy at Salerno in September 1943 that the unit went into action. The landings were almost a disaster and for a brief moment Clark considered evacuating his troops. Dogged perseverance by British and American troops, however, gradually succeeded in pushing back Vietinghoff's German Tenth Army, but it had been a very close call.

Clark was a staff officer of immense ability and a ruthless field commander, able to accept heavy casualties as the price of success. He was highly regarded by his superiors and had many admirers in the British Army, most notably Field Marshal Alanbrooke and Winston Churchill. He was also very ambitious and sought publicity both for himself and his army. He was often suspicious of British motives, fearing that they might steal his limelight. Clark was a brave and energetic general, no stranger to the front line, who tended to fight his battles by the book, adhering tenaciously to tried and tested rules of engagement.

Both armies contained corps and divisional commanders of great experience. Clark's Fifth Army, which fought the first three battles to break the Gustav Line, was a truly multinational unit comprising two American, one British, one French and one New Zealand corps. All of these corps commanders had seen a good deal of active service. **Major General Geoffrey Keyes** (US II Corps) had been Patton's deputy during the Sicilian campaign and took command of II Corps in time for the Volturno crossings. **Major General John P. Lucas** (US VI Corps) had taken over his corps when its previous commander, Major General Dawley, had been relieved following the Salerno landings. Lucas's corps had suffered badly during the Volturno crossings and was withdrawn from the line after the battle to prepare for the landings at Anzio. **Lieutenant-General Sir Richard McCreery** (British X Corps) had been Alexander's Chief of Staff during the African campaign and took over X Corps just before the Salerno landings. Since that time McCreery's corps had suffered heavy losses fighting on Fifth Army's left flank from Naples to the Garigliano. **General Alphonse Juin** commanded the French Expeditionary Corps. It came into the line on 3 January 1944. Juin had been commander of the French North

FAR, LEFT **MajGen Lucian Truscott (left), Commander US VI Corps and LtGen Ira Eaker, Commander US Mediterranean Air Force, at VI Corps' HQ at Anzio. Truscott had commanded US 3rd Division during the Anzio landings and was later promoted to corps commander after MajGen John Lucas was sent home. (US National Archives)**

LEFT **General Wladyslaw Anders, Commander Polish II Corps. Anders was a Polish brigade commander at the start of the war and was captured by the Russians in 1939. He refused to join the Red Army and spent a year in Lubyanka prison, before being released to raise an army of Polish POWs. The Soviets were reluctant to arm these Poles, so Churchill arranged for them to leave Russia and move to the Middle East. Here Ander's men were equipped and trained along British Army lines and then sent to join Eighth Army in Italy. (Imperial War Museum, NA13685)**

African Army and played a major role in bringing his divisions into action on the Allied side during the fighting in Tunisia. New Zealand II Corps was raised just before the second battle for Cassino in February 1944 and was commanded by a redoubtable veteran of both wars with a great list of battle honours. **Lieutenant-General Bernard Freyberg VC** had commanded the Allied forces on Crete during the German airborne invasion in the spring of 1941. He had gone on to lead New Zealand 2nd Division as part of British Eighth Army throughout the campaigns in North Africa and Italy.

British Eighth Army had fought on the right wing of 15th Army Group during the initial campaign in Italy. The bulk of Leese's army was brought across the Apennines for the fourth battle to overcome the Cassino defences and penetrate the Gustav Line. British V Corps was left behind on the Adriatic coast to hold the front there while the three other corps moved into the line alongside US Fifth Army for the final offensive. **Lieutenant-General Sidney Kirkman**, Montgomery's artillery chief at El Alamein, had taken over XIII Corps in January 1944 whilst it was static in the line. **Lieutenant-General Wladyslaw Anders** commanded Polish II Corps. He had led the Poles out of Russia after the long years in captivity and now had the chance to repay his enemy for their rapacious occupation of Poland. **Major-General E.L.M. Burns** commanded the Canadian I Corps that had fought in Sicily and been involved in the heavy fighting north of the Sangro.

GERMAN COMMANDERS

Generalfeldmarschall Albrecht Kesselring, Commander German Army Group C, was a Luftwaffe general. He had fought in World War I with the 2nd Bavarian Foot Artillery Regiment and transferred to the newly raised Luftwaffe in 1932 with the rank of major general. He later led *Luftflotte 1* during the Polish campaign and then *Luftflotte 2* during the Battle of Britain in 1940. He served in Russia before taking command of all land and air forces in the Mediterranean. After the Allied invasion of North Africa, Kesselring was appointed Mussolini's military deputy as well as overall commander of *Luftflotte 2* and Rommel's Panzer Army Africa. His handling of the closing battles of the African campaign

Generalfeldmarschall Albrecht Kesselring, Commander Army Group C and C-in-C German Forces Italy, had served as a Luftwaffe *Luftflotte* commander in Poland, France and Russia. He was then moved to the Mediterranean theatre after the Allied Torch invasion of North Africa as Mussolini's military deputy and became overall commander of Italian forces and Rommel's Panzer Army Africa. (Bundesarchiv, 101/316/1151/12)

RIGHT **GenObst Heinrich von Vietinghoff-Scheel, Commander German Tenth Army.** Von Vietinghoff was a Panzer general who had commanded an armoured division and a Panzer corps in Russia. He formed Tenth Army in Italy in August 1943, just before the Allied invasion. His handling of the defence of the Gustav Line campaign brought him respect from Hitler and he was promoted to take over as C-in-C Italy after Kesselring's move to Germany in April 1945. (Bundesarchiv, 101/314/1012/14a)

FAR, RIGHT **GenMaj Ernst-Gunther Baade (left), Commander 90th Panzergrenadier Division.** Baade's defence of the Cassino position earned him a high reputation among fellow officers and his division's dogged resistance on Montecassino during the first two battles sealed the Allies' fate on the Gustav Line. (Bundesarchiv, 101/315/1110/6)

Luftwaffe GenMaj Richard Heidrich served in France, Crete and at Leningrad before taking command of 1st Parachute Division, which he led in Sicily and southern Italy before it deployed to the Cassino sector in February 1944. Heidrich remained in command until promoted to command I Parachute Corps in early 1945. (Bundesarchiv, 146/76/78/13)

delayed the Axis capitulation by several months and his skilful extraction of his forces from Sicily demonstrated his growing strategic ability. The fighting in Italy and the gradual withdrawal to the Gustav Line marked Kesselring as one of the best tactical generals of the war.

Generaloberst Heinrich von Vietinghoff had commanded German Tenth Army since August 1943, when it was raised in response to the likelihood of an Allied invasion of Italy. He had started the war as leader of 5th Panzer Division and served in the Polish campaign. He later took part in the conquest of Yugoslavia as commander of XLVI Corps, which he then led in Russia as part of Second Panzer Army. Vietinghoff's Tenth Army performed beyond expectations in countering the landings in southern Italy and its commander showed remarkable initiative in resisting the Allies. He conducted a masterful delaying action on the River Volturno and forced Clark's men to fight every inch of the way to the Gustav Line.

Kesselring's other army commander in Italy was **Generaloberst Eberhard von Mackensen**. He had raised the German Fourteenth Army in November 1943 and took it into action against the Anzio landings in January 1944. Von Mackensen was a cavalry general who had performed well in Russia with III Panzer Corps at Rostov and Kharkov and then with First Panzer Army at Stalingrad.

Outstanding among the corps commanders in German Tenth Army was **Generalleutnant Fridolin von Senger und Etterlin.** He commanded XIV Panzer Corps and held the line in front of US Fifth Army during the Cassino battles. Von Senger was a Rhodes scholar at Oxford before World War I and was commissioned into the German Army in 1917. He was a brilliant international horseman and joined the cavalry school in Hanover in 1919. At the outbreak of World War II he commanded the 3rd Cavalry Regiment and saw service in Poland, France and Russia where he led 17th Panzer Division. Further service in the Mediterranean saw him in command of XIV Panzer Corps in October 1943. His handling of this corps during the subsequent battles around Cassino won him great praise and von Senger is recognised as being one of the most able German corps commanders of the war.

OPPOSING ARMIES

The initial battles to break through the Gustav Line at Cassino were fought by the troops of four nations: Germany, America, Britain and France. As the campaign wore on, soldiers of other nationalities were brought into the arena to play their part. From British Eighth Army came divisions from New Zealand, India, Canada, South Africa and Poland. French colonial troops from Morocco, Algeria and Tunisia joined Gen Juin's corps to fight in the mountains of Italy. Other units contributed further to the cosmopolitan nature of the Allied force including the Italian 1st Motorised Division and a battalion of Japanese Americans. Before the fighting in Italy was over in May 1945, units from Brazil and Greece and even Jewish troops from Palestine had joined the struggle. In his final summing up at the end of the war, Alexander could identify 26 countries as having contributed towards the Allied victory. This great array of nations involved in the fighting complicated matters considerably, for each senior commander had to take account of the national sensitivities of his subordinates. Even between great Allies such as the British and Americans, the feathers of national pride could be ruffled by a misplaced order or an unintentional slight. It took a great deal of diplomatic skill from Alexander, Clark and Leese to ensure that all combatants were focussed on fighting the same enemy.

French mule train taking supplies up into the mountains. The absence of any roads or tracks up to the forward positions all along the Cassino front, meant that all supplies had to be portered forward by men and mules. (Imperial War Museum, HU90966)

THE ALLIED ARMY

General Alexander's Fifteenth Army Group consisted of US Fifth Army and British Eighth Army. At the end of 1943 these two armies were struggling up the Italian peninsula, separated by the Apennine Mountains. Allied strategy planned for LtGen Mark Clark's US Fifth Army to make its advance along the coastal plain in the west, while Gen Oliver Leese's British Eighth Army pushed along the Adriatic coast in the east. With the mountains between them, the front line in Italy had been virtually split into two halves. The two armies were thus effectively fighting on separate fronts. On the Adriatic side, British Eighth Army had actually broken through the Gustav Line over the River Sangro, but was unable to advance past Ortona before bad weather closed in and stopped all movement. The Eighth Army had little choice but to remain statically on the defensive through the winter. No more progress could be made on the eastern coastline until the spring. Only Clark's Fifth Army now remained on the offensive.

Sherman tank on display in the centre of Cassino as part of a war memorial to those who died, both civilian and military, during the battles to take Montecassino. (Ken Ford)

Goumier mounted cavalry on their Arab horses, setting out on a reconnaissance patrol. The troops are from 2nd Goum, 2nd Moroccan Division. The picture was taken in the foothills of the Aurunci Mountains after Gen Juin's French Expeditionary Corps had moved across to the Garigliano sector. (Imperial War Museum, NA14155)

US Fifth Army had closed up almost to the Gustav Line by the start of January 1944. LtGen Mark Clark then established his army along the line itself in preparation for the attack. By this time in the campaign, many of the units were in a poor state, worn out by their three months on the offensive and in need of rest and replenishment.

Clark had four corps under his command: US II and VI Corps, British X Corps and the French Expeditionary Corps. US VI and British X Corps had landed at Salerno and had remained in action ever since. The other two corps were still reasonably fresh; US II Corps had joined Clark in November and Gen Juin's French Expeditionary Corps became operational in December. Of these four corps, only three were available for the attempt to break through the Gustav Line. The fourth had already been assigned to a proposed amphibious landing at Anzio, aimed at outflanking the German fortified line. MajGen John Lucas' US VI Corps was the formation chosen for this task. In early January his HQ was pulled out of the line to prepare for the landings and the corps was given two new units with which to make the assault: the US 3rd Division (MajGen Lucian Truscott) and the British 1st Division (MajGen W. Penney).

US II Corps held the centre of Fifth Army's line opposite the Liri valley and Cassino with two National Guard units, the 34th (MajGen Ryder) and 36th (MajGen Walker) Divisions, that had seen a good deal of fighting. Elements of US 1st Armoured Division were in support. On the left of US II Corps, facing the Gustav Line between the Liri valley and the sea was British X Corps made up of 46th Division (MajGen Hawkesworth) and 56th Division (MajGen Templer). Both these formations had fought all the way from Salerno. The British 7th Armoured Division had joined them for a time, but in mid-December the Desert Rats were sent back to England to prepare for the invasion of **21**

France. They was replaced by British 5th Division (MajGen Bucknall) from Eighth Army.

Holding the mountainous right of the line to the north of Cassino was Gen Juin's French Expeditionary Corps. It had two divisions available, the 2nd Moroccan Division (BrigGen Dody) and 3rd Algerian Division (MajGen de Goislard de Monsabert). Most of the troops in these two divisions were Arab, but some were French colonists. Almost all of their officers and NCOs were French. These men were superb mountain troops and fought with great spirit, eager to restore French prestige. They were equipped by the Americans and used American weapons and equipment. They had few transport vehicles of their own, however, and most movement was on foot. The lack of transport was no great disadvantage in the mountain warfare in which they engaged, and their ability to move and fight on almost inaccessible terrain surprised both the Allies and the Germans.

This was the Allied line up for the first of the battles to break the Gustav Line. Clark had just one division in reserve, another National Guard outfit that had seen heavy action; the 45th Division (MajGen Eagles), which was destined to support the Anzio attack. The fighting to take the Cassino position dragged on throughout the early months of 1944 and sucked more and more units into the maelstrom. The first two of the new divisions to be committed to the battlefield were the 2nd New Zealand Division (MajGen Howard Kippenberger) and 4th Indian Division (MajGen F. Tuker). Both of them were from Eighth Army and both were veterans of the North African campaign. The two Divisions were grouped together under the control of a new corps HQ that was raised specifically for the Cassino battles. It was designated II New Zealand Corps and LtGen Sir Bernard Freyberg VC, erstwhile commander of 2nd New Zealand Division, was selected to lead it. British 78th Division (MajGen Charles Keightley) was also brought across from Eighth Army to join II NZ Corps a little later in the struggle.

A German paratrooper shows concern that the end of an Allied artillery barrage might herald another attack on the positions around Montecassino. (Bundesarchiv, 146/91/82/10)

British troops moving across the high mountains close to Cassino. The battlefield was a most inhospitable place: the rubble-strewn landscape made all movement difficult, especially during a night attack and the rocky ground made it impossible to dig in for protection. Shelters, called sangars, had to be built by piling rocks on top of each other. Explosions caused by shell and mortar fire sent razor sharp fragments of rock slicing through anyone unlucky enough to be caught in the open. (Imperial War Museum, IA 18904)

The II New Zealand Corps contained three of Eighth Army's best divisions; all had given a good account of themselves during the fighting in North Africa and all were highly regarded. The 2nd New Zealand Division had seen action in Greece, Crete, Libya, at El Alamein and on the Mareth Line. Since arriving in Italy it had been used to exploit the crossing of the Sangro and the attack on Ortona. Its commander during those battles was LtGen Freyberg, a great hero from World War I where he won the VC and three DSOs, rising to the rank of Brigadier. MajGen Tuker's 4th Indian Division was another of Monty's desert formations. It had begun its war very early and was famous for storming the fortress heights of Keren in Eretrea in 1941 against the Italians. Other battles followed in North Africa including the action at Wadi Akarit. British 78th Division had been part of Anderson's First Army and had helped carry out the assault on Algiers as part of the Torch landings. It performed well in Tunisia, gained further laurels in Sicily and had done much of the fighting on Monty's drive up the Adriatic in Italy, making assault crossings of the Trigno, Biferno and Sangro rivers.

After three attempts to break into the Liri valley past Cassino, the sector was transferred from Fifth Army to Gen Leese and his Eighth Army for the final battle that engineered the collapse of the Gustav Line. Clark's army confined itself to the lower Garigliano sector during this offensive, responsible for the line from the Liri valley to the sea and with the breakout of the Anzio lodgement. This final battle was action on a grand scale and Leese brought many more divisions over the Apennines and introduced new units to the battlefield in order to deliver the knock out punch. British XIII Corps (LtGen Kirkman), consisting of British 4th Division (MajGen Ward), Indian 8th Division (MajGen Russell) and British 6th Armoured Division (MajGen Evelegh), was a veteran outfit with tried and tested methods. Two other new corps also became operational at Cassino: Polish II Corps (LtGen Anders) with Polish 3rd Carpathian Division (MajGen Duch) and Polish 5th Kresowa

Division (MajGen Sulik), and the Canadian I Corps (MajGen Burns) consisting of Canadian 1st Division (MajGen Vokes) and Canadian 5th Armoured Division (MajGen Hoffmeister).

By January 1944, the campaign had degenerated into a slogging match. Each time a river was crossed or a mountain conquered another equally difficult obstacle confronted the advancing Allies. The Allies had superior numbers of guns, tanks, transport and aircraft, allowing the attacks to be well supported. However, the awful weather and difficult terrain were to a degree cancelling out these advantages. The wet winter caused rivers to flood and tracks to be washed away. Often the only means of getting supplies up to the forward troops was by mules or with porters. In the best of conditions Italy was not good tank country and armour could rarely be employed other than in small numbers in an infantry support role. The rain and mud confined almost all armoured movement to metalled roads, of which there were frustratingly few. Overcast skies kept Allied airpower on the ground and, as a result, air support was patchy at best. The war in Italy was decidedly an infantryman's war.

Despite all the hardships, morale in the Allied Armies was still generally relatively high. They were well supplied, supported and armed; stocks of ammunition were adequate and medical facilities excellent. High morale was especially characteristic of the new divisions coming into the line. Those units that had been in action for some time and those with a long list of battle honours from other theatres were, however, more circumspect about the fighting. The winter was harsh, wet and cold. 'Sunny' Italy had never quite lived up to its reputation.

Allied air power in theatre was projected primarily through its Tactical Air Force, commanded by MajGen John Cannon. He had two formations at his disposal: US 12th Air Force, which provided tactical support to US Fifth Army, and the Desert Air Force supporting Eighth Army. The 80 squadrons of fighters, fighter-bombers and medium bombers making up these formations could, when required, be switched between armies at General Alexander's direction. In addition, the heavy bombers of the Mediterranean Strategic Air Force could also be used to support ground troops, under the direction of the Supreme Allied Commander Mediterranean, Gen Wilson. These heavy bombers were based in Italy, Sicily and North Africa and, together with the aircraft of the two tactical air forces, provided a combined operational strength of 3,876 aircraft available in theatre.

ORDER OF BATTLE: ALLIED FORCES

Supreme Commander Mediterranean –
General Sir Henry Maitland Wilson

Fifteenth Army Group – General Sir Harold Alexander

US Fifth Army – Lieutenant General Mark Clark

US II Corps – Major General Geoffrey Keyes
US 34th Infantry Division – MajGen C.W. Ryder
133rd Infantry Regiment
134th Infantry Regiment
168th Infantry Regiment

US 36th Infantry Division – MajGen Fred Walker
141st Infantry Regiment

142nd Infantry Regiment
143rd Infantry Regiment
US 85th Infantry Division – MajGen John Coulter
337th Infantry Regiment
338th Infantry Regiment
339th Infantry Regiment
US 88th Infantry Division – MajGen John Sloan
349th Infantry Regiment
350th Infantry Regiment
351st Infantry Regiment

US 1st Armored Division – MajGen Ernest Harmon
1st Armored Regiment
6th Armored Regiment

British X Corps – LtGen Sir Richard McCreery
British 5th Infantry Division – MajGen Gerard Bucknall
13th Infantry Brigade
15th Infantry Brigade
17th Infantry Brigade

British 46th Infantry Division – MajGen J. Hawksworth
128th Infantry Brigade
138th Infantry Brigade
139th Infantry Brigade

British 56th (London) Infantry Division – MajGen G. Templer
167th Infantry Brigade
168th Infantry Brigade
169th Infantry Brigade

US VI Corps – MajGen John P. Lucas
US 3rd Infantry Division – MajGen Lucian Truscott
7th Infantry Regiment
15th Infantry Regiment
30th Infantry Regiment

US 45th Infantry Division – MajGen William Eagles
157th Infantry Regiment
179th Infantry Regiment
180th Infantry Regiment

British 1st Infantry Division – MajGen W. Penney
2nd Infantry Brigade
3rd Infantry Brigade
18th Infantry Brigade
24th Guards Brigade (attached)

US Ranger Force – Col William O. Darby
1st, 3rd and 4th Ranger Battalions

US/Canadian 1st Special Service Force – BrigGen Robert Frederick

New Zealand II Corps – LtGen Bernard Freyberg VC
New Zealand 2nd Division – MajGen Howard Kippenberger
4th New Zealand Armoured Brigade
5th New Zealand Infantry Brigade
6th New Zealand Infantry Brigade

Indian 4th Infantry Division – MajGen F. Tuker
5th Indian Infantry Brigade
7th Indian Infantry Brigade
11th Indian Infantry Brigade

British 78th Infantry Division – MajGen Charles Keightley
11th Infantry Brigade
36th Infantry Brigade
38th (Irish) Infantry Brigade

French Expeditionary Corps – Gen Alphonse Juin
French 1st Motorised Infantry Division – MajGen Diego Brosset
1st Motorised Infantry Brigade
2nd Motorised Infantry Brigade
4th Motorised Infantry Brigade

Moroccan 2nd Infantry Division – BrigGen André Dody
4th Moroccan Rifle Regiment
5th Moroccan Rifle Regiment
8th Moroccan Rifle Regiment

Algerian 3rd Infantry Division – MajGen de Goislard de Monsabert
3rd Algerian Rifle Regiment
4th Algerian Rifle Regiment
7th Algerian Rifle Regiment

Moroccan 4th Mountain Division – BrigGen François Sevez
1st Moroccan Rifle Regiment
2nd Moroccan Rifle Regiment
6th Moroccan Rifle Regiment

British Eighth Army – Lieutenant-General Sir Oliver Leese

British XIII Corps – LtGen Sidney Kirkman
British 4th Infantry Division – MajGen Dudley Ward
10th Infantry Brigade
12th Infantry Brigade
28th Infantry Brigade

Indian 8th Infantry Division – MajGen Dudley Russell
17th Indian Infantry Brigade
19th Indian Infantry Brigade
21st Indian Infantry Brigade

British 6th Armoured Division – MajGen Vivian Evelegh
26th Armoured Brigade
1st Guards Brigade
61st Infantry Brigade

Canadian I Corps – MajGen E.L.M. Burns
Canadian 1st Infantry Division – MajGen C. Vokes
1st Canadian Infantry Brigade
2nd Canadian Infantry Brigade
3rd Canadian Infantry Brigade

Canadian 5th Armoured Division – MajGen B. Hoffmeister
5th Canadian Armoured Brigade
11th Canadian Infantry Brigade

Army Reserve
South African 6th Armoured Division – MajGen W. Poole
11th South African Armoured Brigade
12th South African Motorised Infantry Brigade

THE GERMAN ARMY

In common with all senior German commanders by this stage of the war, Kesselring suffered from the increasing interference of the Führer, Adolf Hitler. Convinced of his own strategic and tactical genius, and ever more suspicious of the determination and reliability of his commanders in the field, Hitler meddled more and more with the minutiae of military operations, undermining tactical flexibility and limiting the ability of his commanders to respond swiftly to events. One of the few advantages that Kesselring possessed was his simpler and more unified command structure when compared to Alexander's team.

By January 1944 the Commander of Army Group C had 21 divisions in Italy, opposing 18 Allied divisions. Not all of these units were at full strength and some were in need of rest, but the same could also be said for many of the divisions in US Fifth and British Eighth armies. Some of these units were on static duties in the north of the country, whilst others were kept in reserve or were refitting and reforming after fighting elsewhere and as such unavailable for immediate use. Generaloberst von

Vietinghoff's German Tenth Army had 12 divisions with which to hold the entire front along the Gustav Line. These divisions were a mix of first-rate units and other less formidable formations. Many were standard infantry whose ranks had been filled with foreign replacements and who relied on horse-drawn transport. These units were often intended for a largely static defensive role and had, at best, limited offensive capability. Supporting these lesser formations and acting in a mobile 'fire-brigade' role were the Panzer, Panzergrenadier and Fallschirmjäger (parachute) divisions.

German Tenth Army had two corps in the line. XIV Panzer Corps (GenLt Fridolin von Senger und Etterlin) contained eight divisions, three infantry (44th, 71st and 94th) two Panzergrenadiers (3rd and 15th Divisions) and one mountain division (5th Mountain Division). Von Senger's corps held the Gustav Line from the sea in the west to the heights of the Apennine Mountain range. Holding the remainder of the line between the mountains and the Adriatic Sea in the east was LXXVI Corps (GenLt Valin Feurstein) containing 305th and 334th Infantry Divisions, 1st Parachute Division and 26th Panzer Division. Von Vietinghoff had an Army reserve of two mobile divisions held south of Rome, the 29th and 90th Panzergrenadier Divisions. Also near Rome were two Army Group reserves, the *Hermann Göring* Fallschirm Panzer Division (FPzDiv), an elite Luftwaffe armoured division[1], and the 4th Parachute Division.

Generaloberst von Mackensen's Fourteenth Army in northern Italy had the task of guarding against an Allied amphibious landing. Kesselring felt certain that the Allies would use their superiority in naval and air power to form a beachhead somewhere north of the front to destabilise his defence of the country. If they did, von Mackensen would be able to act against it with a mix of infantry and mobile units.

Captured Panzergrenadier from the *Herman Göring* Fallschirm Panzer Division. Part of the division was in action on the Garigliano during the first battle on the Gustav Line and also against US VI Corps' lodgement at Anzio. (Imperial War Museum

---

[1] The 'Fallschirm' (Parachute) designation of the *Hermann Göring* Division was entirely honorific. It had no airborne capability at all, although some former member of Fallschirmjäger units had been incorporated into the formation. It was organised as a conventional Panzer division, although lavishly equipped.

ORDER OF BATTLE: GERMAN FORCES

**Army Group C –
Generalfeldmarschall A. Kesselring**

**German Tenth Army – GenObst Heinrich von Vietinghoff
LXXVI Panzer Corps – Gen der Pz Traugott Herr (On Adriatic Front)**

XIV Corps – Generalleutnant Fridolin von Senger und Etterlin
44th Infantry Division – GenLt Dr Franz Bayer
131st Grenadier Regiment
132nd Grenadier Regiment
134th Grenadier Regiment

71st Infantry Division – GenMaj Wilhelm Raapke
191st Infantry Regiment
194th Infantry Regiment
211th Infantry Regiment

15th Panzergrenadier Division – GenMaj Eberhard Rodt
104th Panzergrenadier Regiment
129th Panzergrenadier Regiment (later designated 115th Pzgrn. Regt.)
115th Panzer Battalion

94th Infantry Division – GenMaj Bernard Steinmetz
267th Infantry Regiment
274th Infantry Regiment
276th Infantry Regiment

29th Panzergrenadier Division – GenMaj Walter Fries
15th Panzergrenadier Regiment

71st Panzergrenadier Regiment
129th Panzer Battalion

5th Mountain Division – GenMaj Julius Ringel
85th Mountain Rifle Regiment
100th Mountain Rifle Regiment

90th Panzergrenadier Division – GenMaj Ernst Baade
200th Panzergrenadier Regiment
361st Panzergrenadier Regiment
190th Panzer Battalion

1st Parachute Division – GenMaj Richard Heidrich
1st Parachute Rifle Regiment
3rd Parachute Rifle Regiment
4th Parachute Rifle Regiment
1st Parachute Machine Gun Battalion

LI Mountain Corps – GenLt Valin Feurstein
When its HQ was transferred from Adriatic front in April 1944, the corps contained 1st Parachute Division, 44th Infantry Division and 5th Mountain Division.

**Fourteenth Army – GenObst Eberhard von Mackensen
LXXVI Panzer Corps – Gen der Pz Traugott Herr**
92nd Infantry Division – GenLt Werner Goeritz
1059th Grenadier Regiment
1060th Grenadier Regiment

362nd Infantry Division – GenLt Heinz Greiner
954th Grenadier Regiment

GenFM Kesselring visiting GenMaj Heidrich and his paratroopers in the Cassino sector. Kesselring was no stranger to the front line and kept in very close touch with all of his commanders right down to battalion level. (Bundesarchiv 101/579/1955/30a)

955th Grenadier Regiment
956th Grenadier Regiment

715th Infantry Division – GenLt Hans-Georg Hildebrandt
725th Grenadier Regiment
735th Grenadier Regiment

114th Jäger (Light) Division – GenMaj Alexander Bourquin
721st Light Regiment
741st Light Regiment

3rd Panzergrenadier Division – GenLt Fritz-Hubert Gräser
8th Panzergrenadier Regiment
29th Panzergrenadier Regiment
103rd Panzer Battalion
Hermann Göring *Fallschirm Panzer Division – GenLt Paul Conrath*
Panzer Regiment *Hermann Göring*

1st Panzergrenadier Regiment *Hermann Göring*
2nd Panzergrenadier Regiment *Hermann Göring*

26th Panzer Division – GenMaj Smilo von Luttwitz
26th Panzer Regiment
9th Panzergrenadier Regiment
67th Panzergrenadier Regiment

1st Parachute Corps – Gen der Fallschirmjäger Schlemm
65th Infantry Division – GenLt Georg Pfeifer
145th Grenadier Regiment
147th Grenadier Regiment

4th Parachute Division – GenMaj Heinrich Trettner
10th Parachute Regiment
11th Parachute Regiment
12th Parachute Regiment

OPPOSING PLANS

By December 1943, it had become clear to Allied commanders that the struggle for Italy was going to be a long drawn out affair. With the enemy using every river and mountain range as a defensive line, there could be no rapid drive on Rome. The new year would bring with it the prospect of attacking the most formidable fortified line of all, the Gustav Line. The advance from Salerno had already been slow and costly both in men and materiel and the coming battle could only prolong this war of attrition. A new way of seizing the initiative had to be found.

THE ALLIED PLAN

The prospect of further amphibious landings in Italy had been the subject of discussion for many weeks. Approval had already been given for the retention of numbers of landing craft in the Mediterranean until the end of January, before they had to be sent back to England ready for the Overlord invasion of France. A plan was proposed, codenamed 'Shingle', for a landing to be made close to Rome at Anzio. This would place Allied forces behind German Tenth Army and allow them to seize the two main roads leading south from the capital. Vietinghoff's army would then have to retreat or be cut off. To divert German forces and help the landings to establish themselves, US Fifth Army would launch an attack against the Gustav Line and advance up the Liri valley before the amphibious assault. This would draw more units of the Tenth Army southwards and reduce the enemy forces available to act against the landings. In effect, the first attack on the Gustav Line would contribute to the success of the Anzio landings, which would in turn threaten German Tenth Army's lines of communication and thus its hold on the Gustav Line.

General Clark was convinced that the Anzio landings would force Vietinghoff to withdraw northwards to avoid his forces being surrounded. To compel the Germans to retreat, however, the US corps at Anzio would have to seize the Alban Hills south of Rome to dominate the two vital roads south. Unless the German commanders panicked, the seizing of the beachhead would not, in itself, be enough.

Major General Lucas was selected to carry out the landings at Anzio with his US VI Corps. The plan was to put two divisions ashore on 22 January

A party of German POWs, probably from 71st Infantry Division, captured by the French on the Garigliano sector in May 1944. (Imperial War Museum, NA14876)

28

1944, supported by British Commandos and American Rangers. Ten days prior to this the French Expeditionary Corps would begin operations into the mountains to the north of Cassino against the Gustav Line. This would be followed by other assaults by other corps elsewhere, steadily increasing the numbers of divisions committed until the whole line was under attack. Lucas would then land his VI Corps in the German rear.

The sector of the Gustav Line in front of US Fifth Army stretched from the sea on the left up into the Apennines on the right. Clark's troops faced a number of physical features that helped buttress the line. The German fortified positions followed the path of the River Garigliano from its estuary to its confluence with the River Liri in the centre. Northwards of this junction, the river was known as the River Rapido. The Liri had formed a wide valley and was dominated on either side by high ground. On the left, the peaks of the Aurunci Mountains separated the valley from the coastal plain, while on the right, the impregnable heights of Montecassino, with its Monastery sitting squarely on its peak, were joined with spurs of high ground that rose to the towering height of Monte Cairo, over 5,000 feet above sea level. The route along the entire valley was dominated by these flanking mountains.

The main road to Rome, Route 6, came up from the south-east into the town of Cassino, which nestled at the foot of Montecassino. It then passed around the base of the mountain and exited into the Liri valley. This was the only road capable of carrying armour and the Liri valley was the only practicable route along which an army advancing on Rome could move. That this single road was dominated by the mountains towering above it presented the Germans with a formidable defensive position. This fact was not lost on them and they had expended great efforts to heavily fortify this sector. Vietinghoff made good use of this high ground, and the superb field of view it gave his artillery observers ensured than every inch of the valley floor was covered by his guns. The fortifications were equally impressive on Montecassino itself, along the valley of the Rapido River that skirted around it and through the town of Cassino. Mines, wire, pillboxes and interlocking mortar and machine gun posts criss-crossed the approaches. The Rapido was dammed and flooded to provide marshy and soft approaches. Cassino and the mountain features surrounding it had been turned into the cornerstone of the Gustav Line defences.

The Allied plan of attack was to assault the Gustav Line almost as soon as Fifth Army arrived. It could not afford to pause and regroup for it had to apply the necessary pressure on the enemy to assist the Anzio landings. The French Expeditionary Force would attack first in a continuation of its move into the mountains to the north of Cassino in the region of the upper Rapido, towards Belmonte Castello and Atina, and then swing southwards into the Liri valley well beyond Montecassino. This attack would be underway by 12 January. Focus would then switch to the south where British X Corps would attack with three divisions across the River Garigliano and into the Aurunci Mountains on 17 January. The corps was not expected to be in position before the 15th, so it would have just two days preparation before the attack. Then the US II Corps would put in the most important assault. It would attack across the Rapido in the Liri valley with one division and form a bridgehead. A combined battlegroup of one infantry and one tank division would then pass through the

Modern view of the River Rapido by Sant Angelo. The village is on the left of the picture with its centre on some high ground overlooking the river. The American assaults by US 36th Division took place both upstream and downstream of this crossing point. (Ken Ford)

bridgehead and strike out towards Rome, linking up with the landings at Anzio en route. The key to success was for the two flank attacks to throw the enemy off balance so that the assault in the centre could achieve the breakthrough.

It was a bold plan that relied on first drawing German reinforcements into the Gustav Line, then that they withdraw to meet the threat to their rear from the Anzio landings. It depended to a great extent on Allied commanders accurately anticipating the actions of their German counterparts. US II Corps might well have to advance up the Liri valley with the heights on both sides still in enemy hands. British X Corps' attack across the Garigliano might seize the heights on the left of the valley. However, Juin's French corps would not seize Montecassino and the heights on the north side of the valley as their planned advance would bypass these positions. Juin would be pushing north-west towards Atina before swinging down into the Liri valley. Success depended on the enemy either pulling back or crumbling under the pressure of the assault.

THE GERMAN PLAN

In formulating his plans Kesselring had the advantages of being able to dictate that the battle would be fought on terrain that was perfect for the sort of defensive battle at which the Germans in Italy had already shown they excelled. In fact it was perhaps the nature of the terrain rather than the forces available to him that formed the basis of Kesselring's planning. Those natural features that dominated the ground over which the Allied advance must pass had been heavily fortified. To achieve a decisive penetration the Allies must take effective control of the Liri Valley. This was the only route by which a breakthrough could be rapidly exploited. The retreat or even collapse of those German forces in the mountains could not be swiftly exploited by the Allies due to the lack of roads down which to pass a force of any appreciable size. The time it would take to push forces forwards would allow the Germans to reorganise, reinforce and occupy the next piece of high ground blocking the advance. Kesselring thus focussed his thinking on the defence of the Liri Valley.

Another factor that worked to Kesselring's advantage was that the two Allied armies fighting their way north were split by the Appenine mountain range. As no significant advance could be made through the mountains themselves, this effectively created two distinct fronts, the Americans in the west and the British in the east. Their operations were not mutually supportive allowing the Germans to deal with attacks on one side of the Appenines and then transfer troops to deal with attacks on the other side. Kesselring had also retained several formations in reserve in the north. Unlike the Allies who were forced to use the high mountain roads over the Appenines, Kesselring had access to the superior road network passing through Rome. These reserves and superior internal lines of communication allowed Kesselring and Vietinghoff to transfer their forces from flank to flank as the fighting dictated. While both armies available to Alexander were in the line, Kesselring had only one of his committed at the start of the Gustav Line offensive; Mackensen's Fourteenth Army was not yet in action, its divisions were ready to move as events dictated.

US FIFTH ARMY'S ATTACK

US Fifth Army's attack against the Gustav Line began with Gen Juin's move onto the high ground north of Cassino on the night of 11/12 January. The French Expeditionary Corps was the right hook of Gen Clark's offensive against the German fortified line. Before actually getting to grips with the Gustav Line, however, the French Corps still had three miles of defended mountainside to cross. General Juin was to send his corps through these mountains attacking towards Belmonte-Castello and Atina, then to swing south and break into the Liri valley well behind the defences at Cassino. Leading the attack was Gen Dody's 2nd Moroccan Division who had already been in action with US VI Corps earlier in December when two regiments of the division had managed to capture the heights of Monte Pantano, an objective that the whole of US 34th Division had been unable to secure a few days earlier. The Berber tribesmen from North Africa had given good account of themselves and had impressed their American masters.

THE FRENCH EXPEDITIONARY CORPS ATTACK

Dody's Moroccan Division attacked in the darkness with all three regiments in line abreast and without any preliminary barrage. The lead battalions stormed across the snow-covered hillsides and penetrated straight into the German positions, making great gains almost immediately. On their left things were a little different as Juin's other unit, 3rd Algerian

Wounded men of the 141st Regiment from the US 36th 'Texas' Division streaming back towards Monte Trocchio after their disastrous attempts to get across the River Rapido. (US National Archives)

The site of 36th Division's attack over the River Rapido, seen from Monte Trocchio. The Texas Division crossed the river in the centre of the picture, to the north of Sant Angelo. The ruined buildings of the village can been seen towards the upper left corner of the picture. (US National Archives)

Division, attacked under the command of GenMaj Monsabert. This was the division's first action and the untried desert tribesmen ran straight into stiff resistance. Its first main objective, Monna Casale, was taken after heavy fighting, but was soon lost again to an enemy counterattack. The summit change hands four times during the day, each attack becoming more frenzied than the previous.

Opposing the French Expeditionary Corps was GenMaj Ringel's 5th Mountain Division and his men were in the process of taking over the line from the 305th Infantry Division when the blow struck. For a while the line wavered and fell back, but the situation soon stabilised as the German mountain troops began to organise themselves in the concrete defences of the Gustav Line proper. They resisted the onslaught with accomplished skill. The fighting in the mountains became protracted and bitter, resolving itself into small unit actions amongst the steep rocks and jagged crags. Both sides were at home in the mountains, France's colonial North Africans pitting themselves against the Bavarian Jägers. The strength of the German defenses eventually proved the equal of the reckless bravery of the *Tirailleurs* and the attacks ground to a halt on 17 January in the sleet and snow of the Italian winter. The two French divisions were now amongst the defences of the Gustav Line and Juin felt that the introduction of one more division into the battle would allow them to break through. Clark was not convinced, however, and he was loath to transfer any American units to the French sector. He had other plans for his divisions, for they were to attack across the lower ground closer to the sea.

The French attack had given the commander of XIV Panzer Corps, GenLt von Senger, some concern, for he knew that he had nothing behind Atina to halt it. If Juin and his men could reach the town, then there would be nothing to stop them pushing south across the mountains to the Liri valley. It was with some relief that von Senger heard the news that the French drive had faltered, for he could now concentrate his forces against the other attacks that had begun over on the Garigliano side of his line.

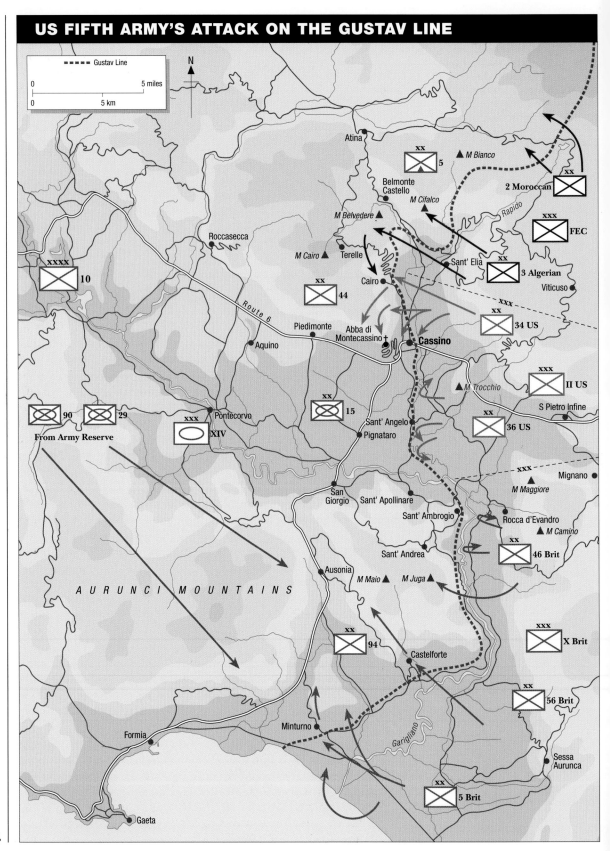

Gustav Line

0 — 5 miles
0 — 5 km

N

Atina

M Bianco ▲

5

Belmonte
Castello

M Cifalco ▲

M Belvedere ▲

2 Moroccan

Rapido

Roccasecca

FEC

M Cairo ▲ Terelle

Sant' Elia

Cairo

3 Algerian

Viticuso

10

44

Route 6

Piedimonte

Abba di
Montecassino †

Cassino

34 US

Aquino

M Trocchio ▲

II US

S Pietro Infine

90 **29**

15

Sant' Angelo

36 US

From Army Reserve

Pontecorvo

Pignataro

XIV

Mignano

M Maggiore ▲

San
Giorgio

Sant' Apollinare

Sant' Ambrogio

Rocca d'Evandro

M Camino ▲

Sant' Andrea

46 Brit

A U R U N C I   M O U N T A I N S

Ausonia

M Maio ▲ M Juga ▲

94

Castelforte

X Brit

56 Brit

Formia

Minturno

Gariglianо

Sessa
Aurunca

5 Brit

Gaeta

BRITISH X CORPS ATTACK

On 17 January British X Corps attacked across the lower Garigliano. The corps had been reinforced by British 5th Division, which had been brought across from Eighth Army. Lieutenant-General McCreery launched his assault with 56th Division in the early evening after a concentrated artillery barrage by the guns of all three of his divisions, plus those of the corps and army artillery. Major-General Templer's London Division, with two brigades in the lead, swept across the river in storm boats opposite Castelforte and secured a bridgehead on the other side. Closer to the sea British 5th Division put in a 'silent' attack. It too assaulted the Garigliano with two brigades, one of which included a seaborne element that tried to land a battalion on the far side of the estuary. Some troops from 2nd Royal Scots were put ashore from landing craft, but extensive minefields kept them bottled up along the shoreline. These minefields also slowed the other attacking battalions and kept them confined to an area close to the far bank.

The enemy holding the opposite side of the Garigliano was German 94th Infantry Division and it put up a stiff resistance to the British assault with artillery and mortar fire. 56th Division took the worst of this and its small gains were achieved at a harsh cost. Over the next two days every attack was met with a counterattack. The German resistance was stiffened by the introduction of a few tanks from the *Hermann Göring* FPzDiv that had been brought down from north of Rome to stifle any breakthrough. The British, however, continued to apply great pressure as more troops were funnelled over the river and into the lodgement. By the end of the second day, X Corps had carved out a significant bridgehead on the lower Garigliano and began to think about advancing over the Aurunci Mountains and into the Liri valley.

Like the French moves in the north, the British attack began to take on an alarming significance to the commander of German XIV Panzer Corps. Von Senger saw the attack as an immediate threat to his defensive line, for if the British continued with their move then his main positions at the mouth of the Liri valley would be outflanked. Von Senger immediately put in a plea to his army commander for the reserves to be released to him and launched against this attack. When the news reached Kesselring he too saw the danger of the move and dispatched his two reserve divisions to Vietinghoff who sent them on to reinforce von Senger's corps. Two crack units, the 29th and 90th Panzergrenadier Divisions, now began their trek down to the Garigliano. In the meantime, 94th Division's strength was bolstered with a regiment from the 15th Panzergrenadier Division, who held the line adjacent to it. With these moves underway, it was inevitable that the British attack would be stopped in its tracks and this is exactly what happened. McCreery's troops were forced to retreat a short way into positions from which they could only conduct an 'active defence'. This move by the enemy was, none the less, exactly what Clark was hoping for. He was drawing on to him the German reserves that could otherwise act against US VI Corps when it landed at Anzio on 22 January.

The other of McCreery's divisions, 46th Division, was due to launch the third of X Corps' assaults across the Garigliano on the right flank, much further up river opposite Sant' Ambrogio. It was planned for 19 January, the attack to take place in conjunction with 128th Brigade – the

View looking north-east across the Rapido Valley from Monte Trocchio. This is the area of the valley to the north of Cassino town over which US 34th Division attacked during the first battle. The area of the Italian barracks is almost dead centre in the picture at the base of the hills, with the small Hill 56 to the right and Point 213 behind. On the right of the picture is the route up to Cairo village. (US National Archives)

Hampshire Brigade – in support of an attack across the River Rapido by US II Corps in the vicinity of Sant' Angelo. The aim was for British 46th Division to divert attention from the site of II Corps' landings and provide some sort of flank protection for the Americans once they were across the river.

The attack by British 46th Division was a disaster. The fast flowing Garigliano first swept away the storm boats and then defied all attempts by the engineers to construct a bridge. Two Hampshire battalions, the 2nd and the 1st/4th, managed to get a few troops over, but all efforts to reinforce them were frustrated by the raging torrent. All 14 separate attempts made to get troops over the river failed. In the morning the division's attack was called off and those men stranded on the far bank were left to their fate.

This failure weighed heavily on the commanders due to launch the US II Corps' assault over the Rapido the next day. With 46th Division's crossing having failed so spectacularly, the Americans would now be entirely unsupported during their attack. Clark briefly considered cancelling the assault, but decided to push on with it because he needed his men in the Liri valley moving towards Rome before the landings got underway at Anzio. The timing was crucial, as only two days were to separate US II Corps' attack and VI Corps' landings.

THE TEXAS DIVISION ON THE RAPIDO

Major General Keyes, the corps commander, had decided to use MajGen Walker's 36th 'Texas' Division for the attack. This veteran National Guard Division had seen a lot of fighting since landing at Salerno, taking heavy casualties in all of its battles. Walker viewed the coming attack with grave misgivings. The approaches to the river were soft and marshy, littered with barbed wire and thick with mines. It would be impossible to get wheeled vehicles forward, so everything, including the rubber dinghies and boats, would have to be manhandled prior to the assault.

Every yard of the approach was under close observation from Montecassino. The river itself was fast flowing with steep muddy banks. On the far side were more minefields and the fixed concrete defences and deep trenches of the Gustav Line, manned by the elite troops of the 15th Panzergrenadier Division. Walker knew that it did not make military sense to attack a water obstacle backed by fixed defences while being overlooked by enemy high ground, but his orders were explicit. He had to form a bridgehead to allow armour to penetrate into the Liri valley. The battle to crack the Gustav Line depended on it.

The attack by the Texans lived up to its commander's worst fears. It was delivered by two of the Division's regiments, 141st Regiment above Sant' Angelo and the 143rd Regiment below the village. Six battalions started their battle at 20.00hrs on the night of 20 January, supported by an artillery barrage on the German positions across the river. The shells did little to silence the enemy grenadiers in their bunkers, for they still harried the Americans all the way to the river with small arms, mortar and machine-gun fire. Through the thick mud the GIs pulled their boats and tried to launch them on the river. Most of the rubber craft were punctured by shellfire and few boats actually took to the water. The small groups of men that did get across were quickly pinned down by enemy fire and the assault stalled. Minor successes were cancelled out by costly failures and disaster reinforced disaster. By the morning only a handful of men remained alive on the far bank.

When Gen Clark received news of the failure he insisted that the Texans try again supported by tanks. The pressure had to be kept up on the enemy. Walker's men did try again and this time managed to get the best part of two battalions across and established two footbridges over the Rapido. Engineers then began the work needed to construct a Class 40 bridge to enable armour to join them, but each time a truck came forward to unload its sections of Bailey it bogged down in the thick mud. Work continued through the night under continual enemy shellfire. By morning the bridge was still not built and successive counterattacks had whittled away the numbers of men on the far side. Daylight on 22 January

An American Stuart light reconnaissance tank knocked out during US 34th Division's attack across the Rapido north of Cassino. (US National Archives)

revealed a hopeless sight. The work on the bridge had been abandoned and the footbridges had been washed away. The men across the river were isolated with no prospect of being reinforced and their small bridgehead was under intense enemy pressure. As the day wore on, less and less news filtered back to 36th Division's HQ until by late afternoon all fell quiet. Those men of the Texas Division across the Rapido River who were not dead had been captured. The attempt to punch directly into the Liri valley had failed on two counts: first it did not achieve a breakthrough into the valley, and second it failed to draw any of the German reserves into the fighting. It was seen at the time by von Senger as nothing more than a spoiling attack, never causing 15th Panzergrenadiers one moment of alarm nor requiring the commitment of any reserves against it.

Although the attack by US II Corps had been turned back, the battles on either flank had unsettled the enemy. They forced Kesselring to commit his two closest reserve divisions and a number of other smaller units to stabilise the threat to the Gustav Line. For a brief moment it looked to the enemy as though the danger had passed, but then US VI Corps came ashore at Anzio.

THE ANZIO LANDINGS

The landings at Anzio took place during the early hours of 22 January. Two divisions, supported by special service forces and armour, landed either side of the town and the neighbouring seaside village of Nettuno. The landings were unopposed. On the left, 2nd Brigade of British 1st Division came ashore to the north of Anzio on Peter Beach, together with 2 Special Service Brigade. Whilst the infantry consolidated its initial lodgement, the

British troops of the 1st Infantry Division make a peaceful landing over the sandy shoreline of Peter Beach, just to the north of Anzio town. The whole division was put ashore on D-Day virtually unopposed. (Imperial War Museum, NA 11041)

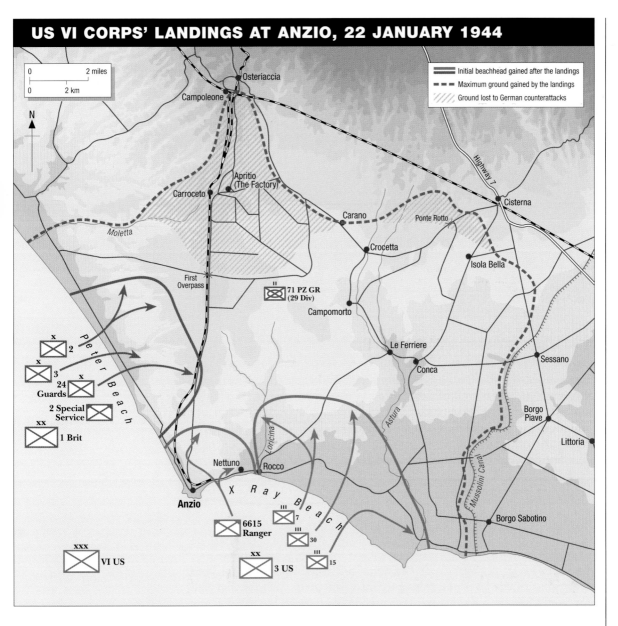

commandos moved to the right to link-up with American forces in the town. 24th Guards Brigade landed behind the assault waves and occupied their preliminary beachhead. In Anzio itself, Colonel Darby's 6615 Ranger Regiment, supported by US 509th Parachute Battalion, landed straight into the town. The Rangers then quickly set about securing the built-up areas and occupying Nettuno. On X-Ray Beach, to the south of Nettuno, US 3rd Division landed all three of its infantry regiments in assault. They too met no major resistance and completed all of their initial objectives without opposition. By noon, the whole of VI Corps was expanding its lodgement to occupy the initial planned beachhead. Behind them, right on target, follow up troops, transport and supplies were being landed over the quiet beaches. The landings were a spectacular success.

Major General Lucas now started to receive congratulatory messages from his commander and from the commander of Fifteenth Army

Tanks of US 1st Armoured Division are unloaded straight onto the waterfront in Anzio, soon after the main landings. (US national Archives)

Group on the his accomplishment, together with a note of caution from Clark to beware of enemy counterattacks. Over the next few days Lucas busied himself with securing his beachhead, which expanded slightly to accommodate the arrival of supplies and equipment and by 24 January the lodgement was seven miles deep and 16 miles wide, carved out against negligible enemy resistance. No plans for a full-scale attack inland had been prepared, however.

When Kesselring heard of the landings just one hour after they had begun he was alarmed, but not surprised. He had anticipated that the Allies would use their superiority in sea and air power to make such an amphibious assault and now it had actually come ashore, he could react appropriately. He quickly decided that the landings would have the Alban Hills as their main objective and realised that if this high ground was taken then it would render the Gustav Line untenable. He immediately despatched the 4th Parachute Division, still not fully assembled, and those units of the *Hermann Göring* Fallschirm Panzer Division that had not been sent south against the Garigliano crossings, to block the route leading from Anzio to the Alban Hills. He then contacted his masters in Berlin and Hitler agreed to release the 715th Division from southern France and 114th Jäger Division from Yugoslavia for use against the landings. Permission was also given for several replacement battalions being raised in the north of the country to be used to activate a new division, the 92nd Division.

Kesselring then turned to his own units and ordered Gen Mackensen to release as many troops as he could towards the landings. Fourteenth Army's commander arranged for 65th and 362nd Divisions, both less one regiment, and elements of 16th SS Panzer Division to move south immediately to counter the Americans at Anzio. This meant that eight divisions, or significant parts of them, were being sent against the landings. None of these units had been withdrawn from the confrontation with US Fifth Army on the Gustav Line. Some of Vietinghoff's units were, however, sent against US VI Corps at Anzio, for Kesselring also requested Tenth

Tank landing ships unloading stores on to the quayside in the harbour at Anzio. The relatively narrow depth of the Allied lodgement meant that the town was within the range of German heavy-calibre artillery, most especially from the large railway gun, 'Anzio Annie' some 15 miles inland. (Imperial War Museum, NA12136)

Army's commander to release all that he could spare. As a result, Vietinghoff withdrew those elements of the *Hermann Göring* Division that had help foil the Garigliano crossings, and released 3rd Panzergrenadier Division (less one regiment) and the 71st Division. He dispatched 26th Panzer Division and some troops from 1st Parachute Division from his forces east of the Appenines.

All this was set in motion by the end of the first day, 22 January. To command and control this gathering of divisions, Kesselring made 1st Parachute Corps operational under GenLt Schlemm. Kesselring had reacted with customary speed and energy. He recognised the dangers posed by US VI Corps' assault and took steps to confine the Americans and British within their small beachhead as a first move to throwing them back into the sea. In contrast with these swift moves to bottle up the landings, it was five days before MajGen Lucas called his divisional commanders to a meeting to discuss plans for taking the offensive 'some time soon.' The main purpose of the landings was to induce the Germans to withdraw Tenth Army from the Gustav Line by vigorous activities in their rear, or at least cause Vietinghoff to thin out his defences by sending units against Anzio. In the event, neither of these objectives was achieved. The Anzio assault was contained mainly by units from elsewhere in Italy and beyond. Tenth Army remained resolutely occupying the Gustav Line in such strength that further operations against it were sure to be costly and prolonged.

THE CASSINO BATTLES

General Mark Clark decided that pressure must be maintained on the Gustav Line to stop German Tenth Army redirecting any reserves against the Anzio landings. If the front was allowed to become too quiet, then Vietinghoff would be sure to redistribute his formations. US Fifth Army would have to continue with the attack until something gave way.

THE FIRST BATTLE FOR CASSINO

On 24 January French Expeditionary Corps and US II Corps both went over to the offensive again, with Gen Juin's colonial troops once more attacking through the mountains to the north of Cassino and Gen Keyes' Americans attempting another crossing of the Rapido at a new site.

General Juin's initial objective was Monte Cifalco, but German 5th Mountain Division clung to its positions and could not be dislodged by the French. The 3rd Algerian Division then side stepped to the left and progressed as far as Monte Belvedere, threatening to outflank the German positions. Fierce enemy resistance and logistical problems soon slowed this ambitious move. Without reinforcement the French Expeditionary Corps lacked sufficient punch to cover the last few miles and achieve a breakthrough. Juin pleaded in vain with Clark for help; none was forthcoming. The Commander of US Fifth Army was too preoccupied elsewhere to appreciate the possibilities of a French victory.

The Benedictine Monastery on Montecassino after Allied air forces had reduced the venerable building to rubble. After the war the Abbey was completely rebuilt and restored to its former glory. (US National Archives)

The rebuilt Benedictine Abbey on the summit of Montecassino as it is today. Picture taken from near Point 450. (Ken Ford)

Juin was left on his own to hold his line and gnaw away at the German defences in the mountains, through the snow, ice and rain.

Down in the valley, Clark's struggle against the Gustav Line continued. With 36th Division now a spent force, MajGen Keyes had to commit II Corps' other division in an attempt to break into the Cassino defences. He planned to put his 34th Division across the Rapido north of the town and get it onto the low hills beyond. His division would then wheel left in a two-pronged assault, with one thrust heading along the high spur towards the Monastery and the other going down the Rapido valley and through Cassino town. The two columns would then pass to the front and rear of Montecassino and into the Liri valley.

The American attack began at the same time as Juin's effort went in on the right up in the mountains. German XIV Panzer Corps' commander, von Senger, had to deal with these two simultaneous assaults on this flank. Initially he was able to leave the defence to his units in the line, playing a waiting game to see how things developed. He had no reserves available to counter any breakthrough, so he had to read the battlefield and be ready to switch resources as they were required. He watched as the two attacks developed and soon decided that the French assault was proving to be the most dangerous. It was to this sector that he diverted the full weight of his artillery and, from their superb observation points, they were able to pin point and break up the French attacks as they developed. In the American sector things proved to be more stable and the 44th Infantry Division were able to contain the assault with the units they had to hand.

The US 34th 'Red Bull' Division attacked across the Rapido in darkness with the 133rd Regiment after a 30-minute barrage. The troops advanced over the flat valley of the Rapido across soft ground inundated by the enemy's damming of the river. Both the approaches to the Rapido and the far side of the river were covered with mines and wire. Progress was initially good and two battalions forded the shallow river and reached the German defences around the ruined Italian barracks. They attacked the enemy with some determination, but when daylight came the Germans in the hills used their superior observation to devastate the Americans with

US field artillery bombarding Monastery Hill after Montecassino had been devastated by Allied bombers in support of New Zealand II Corps' attack during the second battle. (US National Archives)

well placed mortar bombardments and shellfire, forcing the infantry back across the river to their start line. The division tried repeatedly for three days with all three of its regiments to get across the muddy valley and into the hills. Each attack was broken up and each successful crossing of the Rapido was beaten back, yet still the Americans persevered. On 27 January tanks and infantry did managed to get across and stay long enough to enable 168th Regiment to form a small bridgehead. By the 29th this was consolidated and troops moved inland to Points 56 and 213, which were captured that night. German counterattacks failed to regain these important hills and the next day 34th Division pressed on to take the village of Cairo. In their rear, the enemy still held the Italian barracks, but the gains made by 34th Division placed American troops well into the defences of the Gustav Line.

Major General Charles W. Ryder, commander of 34th Division, could now put the second phase of his operation into effect. The 133rd Regiment supported by tanks struck down the Rapido valley towards Cassino, while the other two regiments fanned out along the ridges towards Monastery Hill. Ryder also had the support of 36th Division's 142nd Regiment, which had not been involved in the Texas Division's earlier attack across the Rapido and was still fresh. This regiment was sent up into the mountains on the right to fill the gap between the Americans and the 3rd Algerian Division. It attacked and took Monte Manna after a brilliant advance over treacherous terrain and linked together the flanks of US II Corps and the French Expeditionary Corps.

On the valley floor, the lead battalions of 133rd Regiment pushed their way towards the town of Cassino, but first the enemy-held barracks had to be taken. Fighting for the barracks went on throughout 1 February and into the next day. Eventually the enemy gave up and retreated into the town, helped on their way by the 168th Regiment who were sweeping behind them from Point 213, placing them in great danger of being outflanked. Then 133rd Regiment pushed on down the road and into the buildings on the northern edge of Cassino. Tanks and infantry pounded away at the German defences, but no sooner was one position taken than another opened up. The Americans got into outlying buildings and fought for several days with fanatical determination, but never succeeded in penetrating more than a few hundred yards into the town.

On the hills and mountains above Cassino, 135th and 168th Regiments pushed on along the spurs that led towards Montecassino. 142nd Regiment handed over Monte Manna to the French, wheeled south and joined the advance. Taking one high point after another, the men of the Red Bull Division and the Texans edged closer to the elusive breakthrough.

By this time von Senger had become very worried about the American advance. He could see that if it reached Monastery Hill the Americans would look down into the Liri valley and could blow a wide gap in the Gustav Line. His 44th Division was becoming tired and fragmented as the Americans opened up cracks in its defences. Von Senger felt his hold on the line slipping; he had to bring some fresh impetus into the defence, but he knew that he could expect little help from Tenth Army reserves; all available units were going into the line around Anzio. He decided to switch strong elements of his 90th Panzergrenadier Division, under the capable command of GenMaj Ernst Baade, from the line opposite British X Corps across to the Cassino sector. He had correctly deduced that Clark's main effort had shifted from the Garigliano sector to the mountains above Cassino.

The American attacks across the mountains behind Cassino continued through the first few days of February. Moving from one pile of rocks to another, the three regiments advanced at a snail's pace across a barren moonscape. The enemy was always above them on higher peaks, always

Italian 194mm railway gun of 269th Battery, Italian 1st Armoured Artillery, firing in support of Allied troops in Cassino. This battery was the only one from the regiment that had escaped the German takeover when Italy surrendered. With a range of over ten miles it was a useful addition to Allied firepower. (Imperial War Museum, NA 12848)

AMERICAN INFANTRY AND TANKS ATTACK ACROSS THE RAPIDO VALLEY DURING THE FIRST BATTLE FOR CASSINO.
(pages 46–47)

With the US 36th Division having failed to get across the River Rapido and into the Liri valley south of Cassino, MajGen Ryder was ordered to make an attack over the river to the north of the town with his 34th Infantry Division. Ryder's unit was a National Guard division raised mainly in Minnesota and the Dakotas. Its divisional patch was a red buffalo's skull on a black background (1) giving it the nickname of the 'Red Bull' Division. Its men were among the first to be sent across the Atlantic to Britain after the US joined the war and the division took part in the North African landings in Algeria in November 1942. Ryder selected his 133rd Regiment to carry out the operation, with its 1st and 3rd Battalions attacking across the valley towards the area of the Italian barracks between the river and the mountains. With the river valley dominated by the mountains to the rear, the Germans could observe all activity in front of Cassino with ease. Monastery Hill (2) towers above both the Rapido and Liri valleys, while Point 435 – Hangman's Hill (3) – guards its southern slopes. To the right, Point 593 – Snakeshead Ridge (4) – bars the route towards the Abbey across the mountains from the north. Close above the town, the medieval ruins on top of Castle Hill (5) cover the direct route up to the summit of Montecassino from the east. The 133rd Regiment's attack was supported by the 54 medium and 17 light tanks of the US 756th Tank Battalion. Here an M4A3 Sherman (6) from

the battalion has bogged down in the soft ground. The start line for the operation was over a mile away from the river Rapido near the village of San Michele. The Americans had to advance across the valley floor, liberally sown with mines, over ground that had been flooded by the Germans by diverting the natural course of the river (7). The attack started at 22.00hrs on 24 January with little success. Exploding mines disorientated the troops and the tanks became bogged down in the mud, some infantry reached the river but could not establish themselves because of enemy fire. The next day, MajGen Ryder introduced the remaining battalion of the 133rd Regiment, the 100th Battalion, into the attack. This attempt also failed. Further attempts were made over the following days, with more infantry and more tanks being introduced into the battle until Ryder had nine battalions of infantry and three battalions of tanks committed to the operation. Eventually, on 29 January, the division did get troops established over the Rapido and into the village of Cairo. Then began the lengthy struggle to gain entry into Cassino (8) and to advance across the hills behind the town towards Monastery Hill. It is interesting to note that the 133rd Regiment's 100th Battalion was composed of over 1,500 Nisei Americans of Japanese descent, mainly from Hawaii's National Guard. In September 1943 this battalion replaced the regiment's original 2nd Battalion. The enlistment of Japanese Americans into combat units was controversial, but the battalion was eventually to earn itself an enviable reputation in battle. (Howard Gerrard)

with the better observation, shelling and mortaring the advance. The Americans were made to pay a heavy price for the small gains they made along the two spurs of Snakeshead and Phantom Ridges. The weather was appalling; bitterly cold winds, flurries of snow and sleet and sharp frosts gradually wore down the men' physical resistance. There was no shelter to be had, piles of stones and clefts in the rocks provided the only cover from the elements and the enemy.

By 4 February the men on the mountains had exhausted themselves. For three days there was a pause and it was the turn of the artillery and mortars to harass the enemy. Then on 7 February Clark ordered a final assault be made to capture Montecassino itself and break into the Liri valley. The whole of 36th Division would be put into the attack along with 34th Division. In support, and to divert the enemy's attention, McCreery's X Corps would attack in the south and Juin's FEC would resume its advance in the north. The French and British flank attacks against the Gustav line achieved little. Both McCreery's and Juin's men were exhausted and lacked the power to make a penetration. At Cassino 133rd Regiment hammered away at the town on the valley floor and the other Regiments made one last push onto the high points that dotted the hills behind the town. Looking down on every move was the Monastery and the enemy. Monte Castellone, Monte Maiola, Points 706, 481, 445, 475, 593 and 175 all saw fighting on and around them. Some were captured and then had to be given up. Others were never secured although troops had gained their summits. The fluid nature of the fighting and the close proximity of each side resulted in a front line that changed almost by the hour. Points 450 and 445 were briefly taken and a final push made it almost to the walls of the Monastery, but, like all of the other attacks, it failed. There was just not sufficient strength to make the decisive push. Heroism and will power alone were not enough to secure victory. The enemy, the weather and the terrain had beaten the Americans. The attack was called off and the troops withdrew into more tenable positions on the exposed mountains. US Fifth Army had shot its bolt. All of its divisions had tried, but the Gustav Line had beaten them. The first battle for Cassino was over; it was now time for new a formation to take up the assault.

ATTEMPTED BREAK OUT FROM ANZIO

While this latest attempt was being made on the Gustav Line, events in the Allied beachhead at Anzio were unfolding at a slow pace. Four days after the landings Lucas was still preparing to make his move. This delay convinced Kesselring that the amphibious attack was being commanded by a cautious methodical general unlikely to launch an aggressive and daring breakout. To capture the Alban Hills the Allied forces would have had to attack much earlier, before German forces were in position to counter such a move. Kesselring was comfortable that he faced an orthodox and predictable strategist, and that US VI Corps' objective would be to cut Tenth Army's lines of supply and communication by seizing Cisterna on Route 7 and Valmontone on Route 6. He therefore directed the first divisions of Mackensen's Fourteenth Army to arrive in the area to concentrate at Cisterna, which would be VI Corps' first objective.

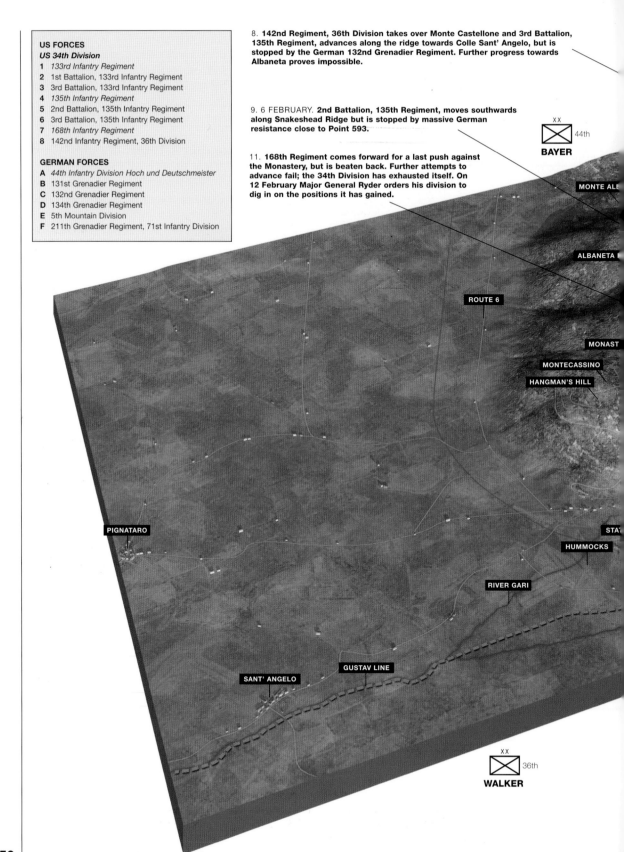

US FORCES

US 34th Division

1 *133rd Infantry Regiment*
2 1st Battalion, 133rd Infantry Regiment
3 3rd Battalion, 133rd Infantry Regiment
4 *135th Infantry Regiment*
5 2nd Battalion, 135th Infantry Regiment
6 3rd Battalion, 135th Infantry Regiment
7 *168th Infantry Regiment*
8 142nd Infantry Regiment, 36th Division

GERMAN FORCES

A *44th Infantry Division Hoch und Deutschmeister*
B 131st Grenadier Regiment
C 132nd Grenadier Regiment
D 134th Grenadier Regiment
E 5th Mountain Division
F 211th Grenadier Regiment, 71st Infantry Division

8. **142nd Regiment, 36th Division takes over Monte Castellone and 3rd Battalion, 135th Regiment, advances along the ridge towards Colle Sant' Angelo, but is stopped by the German 132nd Grenadier Regiment. Further progress towards Albaneta proves impossible.**

9. 6 FEBRUARY. **2nd Battalion, 135th Regiment, moves southwards along Snakeshead Ridge but is stopped by massive German resistance close to Point 593.**

11. **168th Regiment comes forward for a last push against the Monastery, but is beaten back. Further attempts to advance fail; the 34th Division has exhausted itself. On 12 February Major General Ryder orders his division to dig in on the positions it has gained.**

XX
44th
BAYER

MONTE AL

ALBANETA

ROUTE 6

MONAST

MONTECASSINO

HANGMAN'S HILL

PIGNATARO

STA

HUMMOCKS

RIVER GARI

GUSTAV LINE

SANT' ANGELO

XX
36th
WALKER

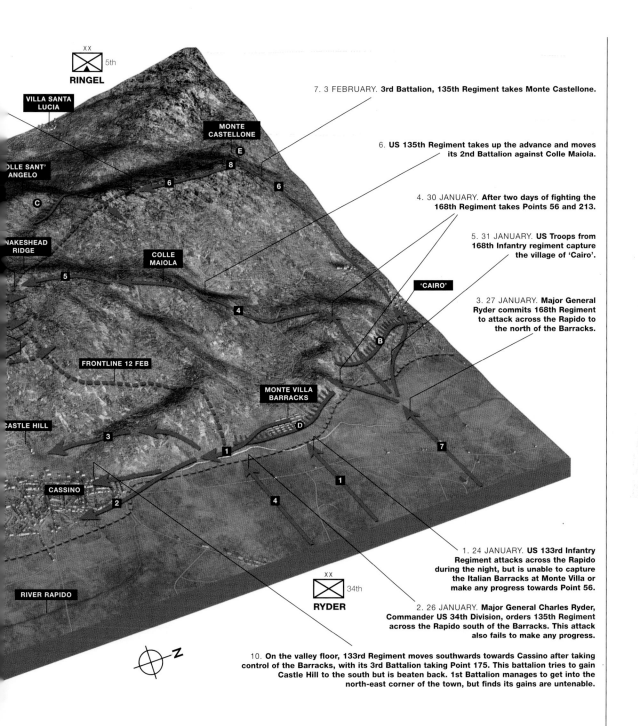

XX 5th
RINGEL

VILLA SANTA LUCIA

MONTE CASTELLONE

7. 3 FEBRUARY. **3rd Battalion, 135th Regiment takes Monte Castellone.**

E
8

OLLE SANT' ANGELO

6

6

6

6. US 135th Regiment takes up the advance and moves its 2nd Battalion against Colle Maiola.

C

4. 30 JANUARY. **After two days of fighting the 168th Regiment takes Points 56 and 213.**

NAKESHEAD RIDGE

COLLE MAIOLA

5

5. 31 JANUARY. **US Troops from 168th Infantry regiment capture the village of 'Cairo'.**

4

'CAIRO'

B

3. 27 JANUARY. **Major General Ryder commits 168th Regiment to attack across the Rapido to the north of the Barracks.**

FRONTLINE 12 FEB

MONTE VILLA BARRACKS

CASTLE HILL

D

3

1

7

CASSINO

2

1

4

XX 34th
RYDER

RIVER RAPIDO

1. 24 JANUARY. **US 133rd Infantry Regiment attacks across the Rapido during the night, but is unable to capture the Italian Barracks at Monte Villa or make any progress towards Point 56.**

2. 26 JANUARY. **Major General Charles Ryder, Commander US 34th Division, orders 135th Regiment across the Rapido south of the Barracks. This attack also fails to make any progress.**

N

10. **On the valley floor, 133rd Regiment moves southwards towards Cassino after taking control of the Barracks, with its 3rd Battalion taking Point 175. This battalion tries to gain Castle Hill to the south but is beaten back. 1st Battalion manages to get into the north-east corner of the town, but finds its gains are untenable.**

US II CORPS' ATTACK NORTH OF CASSINO
24 January–12 February 1944, viewed from the southeast, showing US 34th Division's unsuccessful attempt to push through the mountains to the north and break into the Liri Valley behind Cassino.

Polish infantry from 3rd Carpathian Division getting supplies up to their forward positions over the rear face of Snakeshead Ridge. Everything used in the fighting had to be manhandled up to the front across near vertical rock faces and all movement in areas facing the enemy could only take place at night. (Imperial War Museum, MH1978)

Kesselring could not believe his luck. The Americans in the Anzio beachhead had made no attempt to attack him and now he was gathering his forces for a counterattack that would push the landings back into the sea. There had been contact all along the perimeter and some heavy clashes and exchanges of territory had occurred, but the Americans had made no major push. On 30 January von Mackensen gave orders for his counterattack to begin the following day and it looked as if the Germans would be the first to strike. MajGen Lucas beat him by 24 hours.

On the ninth day of the landings Lucas finally made his move and began to attack out of his beachhead. The follow-up US 45th Division held the flanks of the landings while US 3rd Division and British 1st Division, together with the tanks of the US 1st Armored Division, Rangers and a detachment of paratroops, struck out of the perimeter. On the left the British advanced towards the Alban Hills and actually gained 2,000 metres of ground in two days of fighting before they were stopped by overwhelming enemy resistance. On the right, the Rangers led an attack towards Cisterna. They ran into the *Hermann Göring* Division holding a defensive line in front of the town. Two battalions of Darby's Rangers were virtually wiped out. On either side of this attack, 3rd Division was also halted by well-entrenched German troops. They attacked again the next day and some progress was made and ground taken, only to be given up when the enemy counterattacked with Tiger tanks. The drive was halted and both sides slugged it out, each trying to break the other's resolve. On the third day, 1 February, the Americans tried again with the same results; Cisterna still eluded them. MajGen Truscott, commander US 3rd Division, realised that he was now opposed by forces that were numerically stronger, for every day that had passed had seen new German formations fed into the line. It was clear to Truscott that the enemy was gathering for a major counterattack. He knew that if this attack fell on his now tired division the results would be disastrous, with every probability that his division would be pushed back into the sea. He called a halt to his advance and went over to the defensive, ordering his troops to dig in and prepare themselves for whatever the Germans were about to throw at them. Lucas agreed; it was time for his corps to brace itself for the enemy onslaught.

THE NEW ZEALAND CORPS AND THE SECOND BATTLE FOR CASSINO

Alexander took the decision to bring new divisions across to the Fifth Army front in late January. Clark's army had committed all of its divisions and had no fresh formations other than a combat command of US 1st Armored Division who were in reserve ready to exploit any breakthrough. The Adriatic front was at that time static, for the enemy, the weather and the terrain had all conspired to halt Gen Leese's advance up the east coast of Italy, just as they had halted Clark in the west. Alexander therefore decided to switch three of Eighth Army's divisions to the west. He moved 2nd New Zealand Division, 4th Indian Division and British 78th Division across the Apennines and assigned them to Clark's Fifth Army. The first two of these divisions arrived in late January and early February and were available for use by Clark during II Corps attack through the mountains towards Monastery Hill. He chose not to use them. The 78th Division did not arrive in the area until 17th February. These units were grouped together into a new corps, designated II New Zealand Corps, which was placed under the command of LtGen Bernard Freyberg VC, the long time commander of 2nd New Zealand Division. Freyberg's old division was handed over to one of its longest serving brigade commanders, Howard Kippenberger. Clark now had five corps in his Fifth Army, only two of which were American.

A German paratrooper relaxing in his well camouflaged trench on the hills above Cassino, during a respite in the battle. (Bundesarchiv, 146/32/18/12a)

Both the New Zealand Division and the 4th Indian Division came with impressive reputations. The two divisions had performed exceptionally well with Eighth Army and their commanders were highly regarded. With this new corps Gen Clark could contemplate a fresh attack on the Gustav Line, both to engineer a break-through and to maintain pressure on Kesselring to stop him moving against Anzio. The plan for using the corps was virtually a continuation of US II Corps' attack that had petered out on 11 February. Keyes's men had almost reached the Monastery in their last attempt, which had faltered just one mile from the Liri valley. Senior officers were convinced that the introduction of two fresh divisions into the attack might be just what was required to cover that last extra mile. To bolster the assault, Freyberg requested the use of tactical fighter-bombers in support of the ground troops.

Not everybody thought that this was the best use of the corps. General Juin, quite naturally, suggested that the new corps should be used to add impetus to his attack and drive for Atina and then swing left down into the Liri valley in order to outflank the Cassino position. With hindsight, he may well have been right. Major-General Tuker, Commander 4th Indian Division, was in agreement with this move through the mountains,

r that his division had battalions of Gurkhas from the mountains
ll who would relish that type of warfare. There was much to
...mend this course of action, but it was eventually rejected as being logistically unsound. Keeping several divisions supplied by mule trains through high mountains thick with snow and ice would be very risky. Freyberg agreed, he decided that the direct paths through Monastery Hill and Cassino against the strongest of the enemy's defences would be the route that offered the best prospects.

The operation was due to begin on 16 February and Freyberg planned a two-pronged attack on the town of Cassino and Montecassino. 4th Indian Division would take over the positions of US 34th Division overlooking Monastery Hill and 2nd New Zealand Division would occupy the valley in front of the town. The Indians would then resume the advance begun by US II Corps and the New Zealanders would attack from the east along the railway line towards the railway station using infantry and tanks. They would first have to cross the Rapido and so its engineers would have to bridge the river and several cratered areas along the railway embankment. Freyberg's plan, to continue the attack across a hostile and well defended mountainside and couple it with yet another crossing of the Rapido was not very imaginative, but it seemed to be the best option available.

When the men of 4th Indian Division went up into the mountains to relieve US 34th and 36th Divisions they found things were not as expected. Contrary to the briefing they had received from US II Corps, the Americans did not hold Snakeshead Ridge and the key location of Point 593 along its spine was still in German hands. Matters were made worse when Gen Baade's men launched a counterattack and took back more of the ground that the Americans had held. The consequence was that before 4th Indian Division could launch its assault on Monastery Hill it now had to clear its proposed start line, which included the dominating feature of Point 593.

When MajGen Tuker saw the ground over which his division was to attack he was convinced that the battle plan was seriously flawed. Every yard of the ground that his men would have to cross was covered by interlocking fields of fire from enemy positions. Every approach to the summit of Montecassino and its religious building was overlooked by higher ground. The most direct routes from Points 450 and 445 would be the most deadly whilst any part of Snakeshead Ridge was held by the Germans, for the attacking troops would have the enemy in front, to the right and to the rear of them. The Americans had discovered the truth of this when all of their attacks were stopped dead with horrific casualties. Snakeshead Ridge, and Points 593 and 569 along it, would have to be taken first and the only means of achieving this was to advance along its narrow length on a very confined front, with room to deploy no more than one company at a time. Tuker knew that the proposed attack was unsound and expressed his view that the effort should be made further to the north from Gen Juin's positions. His views were rejected.

Tuker was also unhappy about the Monastery, for it looked down on everyone in the Cassino sector from its dominating position. Research by the general had discovered that it had been built like a fortress, with solid masonry walls 150ft high and ten feet thick at their base. There were loopholes and small windows along its sides and battlements along

Snakeshead Ridge runs across the skyline in this view from just below the walls of the Monastery. On the left end of the ridge is the stony outcrop of Point 569, with the stark white Polish War Cemetery below on the slopes of Points 444 and 450. To the right of Point 569 is the monument which marks point 593, the unassailable height that the Germans refused to relinquish. To the right of the picture is Point 476. (Ken Ford)

the top of its wall. It was from every angle a formidable defensive strongpoint. But it was a strongpoint that was supposed to be inviolate. The Nazis had proclaimed a 300m 'neutrality zone' around it to protect the venerable building, and gave orders that none of their troops were to enter it. As the fighting grew nearer, however, the protected zone shrunk until von Senger ordered positions to be constructed right up against its walls. The American troops on the ground around the Monastery were convinced that there were German observers in the Abbey using it as a spectacular observation post. Several reports from civilians said that they had seen Germans within its walls. This was even confirmed by the American air force general, Ira Eaker, who had flown over the building and claimed to have seen a radio aerial and soldiers moving in and out of the building.

MajGen Tuker felt that his men were at a distinct disadvantage with respect to the Monastery. Allied orders prohibited any shellfire to be aimed at the building and yet the enemy was dug in beneath its walls in prepared positions and reinforced caves. How long would the inviolate nature of the building be respected if his troops actually fought their way up to the building itself? Would they then find that the enemy had gone inside and turned the Monastery into a fortress, or would they keep their word and withdraw down into the Liri valley leaving the way open to Rome? In Tuker's mind it came down to a question of the lives of his men against the sanctity of a building. He made a request to Freyberg that a bombing raid against the Monastery and the German positions on the top of Montecassino precede his attack.

Tuker's request began a long dialogue in the Allied high command, the commanders well aware of the momentous and controversial nature of the choice facing them. Whatever the outcome of the battle, the destruction of the ancient building would lead to charges of vandalism throughout the free world. Freyberg agreed to Tuker's request and put it to Clark. General Mark Clark was against the bombing but agreed to it as a military necessity as did General Alexander. General Wilson sanctioned the bombing and released the full weight of Allied bomber forces to bombard the Monastery. The ancient Abbey's fate was now sealed.

Lieutenant-General Freyberg's attack was due to take place on 16 February and it was important that this start date was kept. Allied intelligence had discovered this was also the planned date of von Mackensen's counter-attack against the Anzio lodgement. It was therefore vital that pressure be maintained on the Gustav Line to occupy Vietinghoff's Tenth Army and prevent forces withdrawing to aid von Mackensen. The employment of bombers against Cassino meant they would be unavailable to help US VI Corps resist German Fourteenth Army's attack. Therefore, the bombing of the monastery had to be brought forward to 15 February to allow the aircraft to operate over Anzio on the 16th.

This change of date exacerbated the problems being faced by 4th Indian Division. The faulty information they had received about American positions in the mountains and the difficulties experienced in taking over their positions left the Indian Division with little time to prepare itself for the battle. Further mis-fortune befell the division when its commander became ill and had to be evacuated. Major-General Tuker was replaced by Brigadier Dimoline. The brigadier protested to Freyberg that he could not start his attack proper until Point 593 had been taken, and he needed more time to arrange this. His request was refused; the attack against Monastery Hill had to begin on 15 February immediately after the bombing. Any further delays would be unacceptable, pressure on the enemy had to be maintained. Dimoline would have to take Point 593 and launch his attack at the same time. This decision left Dimoline with an almost impossible task.

142 heavy and 114 medium bombers destroyed the ancient Benedictine Abbey on the summit of Montecassino on the morning of 15 February. The giant blockbuster bombs dropped on the venerable building reduced it to a pile of rubble. The massed carpet-bombing killed scores of Italian civilians who were taking refuge in the Monastery and many more Germans in positions amongst the hills. The bombing also killed 40 men of the Indian Division in their shelters along the mountainside. The Monastery had gone and with it the restrictions; all-out war could now descend on Montecassino.

The weight of explosives dropped on Monastery Hill left the German defenders dazed and shocked. They were disorientated in the rubble-strewn moonscape and clearly vulnerable to an attack launched against them. Their nightmare continued when all available Allied guns took up the fight and pounded the area with artillery shells. By mid afternoon it should have been the time to launch the assault. Unfortunately, nothing materialised until, under the cover of darkness one company of 1st Royal Sussex Regiment, three officers and 63 men, slipped out from their refuges and moved against Point 593. The greatest bombing raid of the war so far launched in support of ground troops was being followed by an attack by less than 70 men. The results were not spectacular.

General Alexander (right) during a visit to the Anzio beachhead inspects the damage being inflicted by constant long range German artillery fire. (Imperial War Museum, NA11883)

The attack made by the Royal Sussex Regiment was beaten off with heavy losses. Further attempts were rebuffed with equally severe punishment. The next night men of the Royal Sussex tried again with the rest of the battalion. Despite hand-to-hand fighting and great acts of bravery the attack was beaten back by the enemy. The following night, under great pressure from Freyberg, the commander of 7th Indian Brigade, Brigadier Lovett, was reinforced and ordered to make a five battalion attack directly towards Montecassino through Points 444 and 450, whether he captured Point 593 or not. On 17 February Lovett tried again as ordered, leading with 4th/6th Rajputana Rifles against Point 593, 1st/2nd Gurkhas against Point 444 and with 1st/9th Gurkhas attacking Point 450. The Rajputs failed to take 593 and, as foreseen by Brig Lovett, the Gurkhas were caught in enfilade by the German defenders and pinned down on the bare mountainside. The 1st/2nd Gurkhas did make it down the ravine below Monastery Hill and tried to climb up to the Abbey, but were beaten back with great loss. As daylight came, the survivors of all three attacking battalions were back on their start lines with nothing to show for their efforts save a landscape littered with bodies.

Down on the valley floor to the east of Cassino 2nd New Zealand Division put its attack in on the town on the night of 17 February. Kippenberger had planned for 28th (Maori) Battalion to advance along the railway embankment from the east, cross the Rapido and seize the railway station and the area of Cassino close by Route 6. Engineers would then bridge the river and fill the gaps blown in the embankment to allow tanks over to join up with the Maoris. This small lodgement within the Gustav Line would then be exploited by a thrust around the base of Montecassino and into the Liri valley.

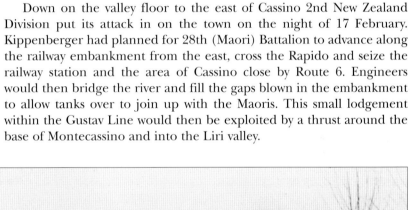

American Rangers attack an Italian farm on the edge of the Anzio lodgement. The man on the left is using a hand held anti-tank rocket launcher, a 'Bazooka,' against the building. (US National Archives)

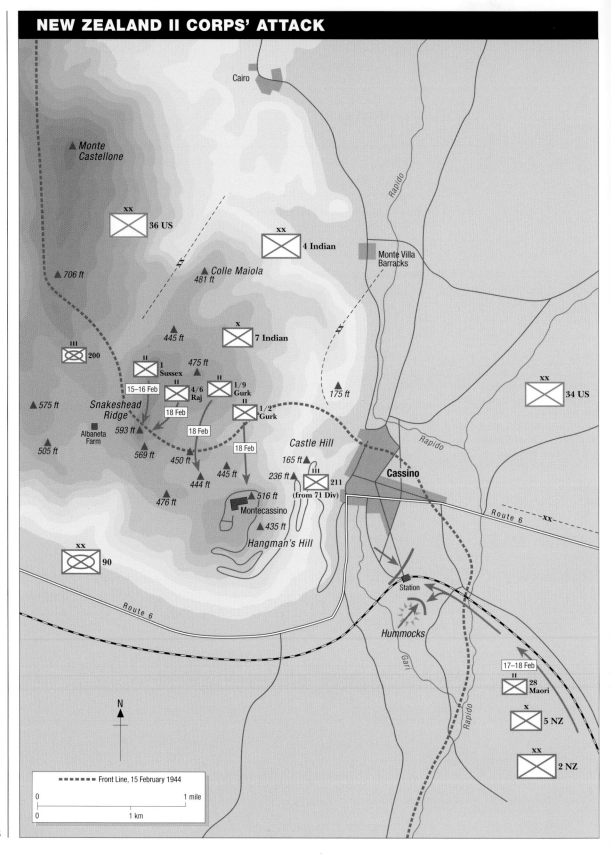

▲ Monte
Castellone

Cairo

xx 36 US

Rapido

▲ 706 ft

▲ Colle Maiola
481 ft

xx 4 Indian

Monte Villa
Barracks

▲ 445 ft

x 7 Indian

▲ 575 ft

III 200

II 1 Sussex

▲ 475 ft

15–16 Feb

II 4/6 Raj

II 1/9 Gurk

xx 34 US

Snakeshead
Ridge

18 Feb

18 Feb

II 1/2 Gurk

▲ 175 ft

Albaneta
Farm

593 ft ▲

18 Feb

Castle Hill

Rapido

▲ 505 ft

▲ 569 ft

450 ft ▲

18 Feb

165 ft ▲

III 211
(from 71 Div)

Cassino

444 ft ▲

▲ 445 ft

236 ft ▲

▲ 476 ft

▲ 516 ft

Montecassino

Route 6
xx

xx 90

▲ 435 ft

Hangman's Hill

Station

Route 6

Hummocks

Gari

17–18 Feb

II 28 Maori

x 5 NZ

Rapido

xx 2 NZ

N

```
------ Front Line, 15 February 1944
0                              1 mile
0                  1 km
```

The 28th Battalion attacked at 21.30hrs and despite enemy resistance, barbed wire and minefields, fought its way through to the railway station and occupied the building, the engine sheds and nearly succeeded in seizing an important knoll to the south known as the Hummocks. Behind them, throughout the night, sappers worked feverishly on constructing a route for the tanks. They bridged one gap after another and bulldozed craters and obstructions that barred their way, but one large gap defeated them. Daylight came and exposed the vulnerable engineers to accurate and persistent enemy shellfire. All work on the construction of the causeway had to stop. This left the Maoris alone and unsupported. Without armour their hold on the station was precarious in the extreme. Smoke was put down to shield them from enemy artillery fire, but the enemy used this as cover for its own counterattack. When the Germans struck during the late afternoon the Maoris were evicted from the station and forced to withdraw back to their start line. Both attacks by II New Zealand Corps had now failed. Freyberg called a halt while he prepared his next plan – the second battle for Cassino was over.

The German Counterattack at Anzio

Whilst Gen Clark's Fifth Army was conducting its latest attempt to get behind Cassino with II New Zealand Corps, the Germans were striking back at the Anzio beachhead. Von Mackensen had launched his counteroffensive against US VI Corps at Anzio and initially made very good progress. German Fourteenth Army had several powerful units deployed against the Allied lodgement and launched them in a devastating attack on either side of the Anzio–Albano road. On 16 February 1st Parachute Corps (4th Parachute Division and 65th Division) moved down the west side of the road while LXXVI Panzer Corps (Lehr Regiment, 3rd Panzergrenadier Division, 114th Jäger Division and 715th Division) attacked down the eastern side. 26th Panzer and 29th Panzergrenadier Divisions waited in support ready to exploit any breakthrough. Against them, spread throughout the beachhead, were British 1st and 56th Divisions, together with US 3rd and 45th Infantry Divisions and 1st Armored Division, supported by Special Forces units.

When the German blow struck, the Allied line faltered and the enemy made early gains. Allied artillery and aircraft replied to this German onslaught, however, and helped to redress the balance. At the end of the first day von Mackensen had had the best of the battle, forcing the Allies back towards their final beachhead line, beyond which they could not retire. The second day of the fighting continued in the same way, with each sides slugging it out at close quarters. The Germans forced a gap through the lines of US 45th Division and sent 14 battalions of infantry and tanks attacking towards the sea. Lucas brought forward his reserves to plug the opening and then hit the Germans with a bomber attack against their concentrations in the rear. On the third day von Mackensen decided to commit his two reserve divisions, but the Americans steadfastly broke up each attack with their massed artillery and the line held. Further German attacks on the 19th attempted to consolidate the gains already made but without success. In the afternoon Lucas actually launched a counterattack backed with tanks and succeeded in pushing the enemy back a mile from the final defensive line. By the next day, both sides had completely exhausted themselves. A few further small attacks were put in but all failed and von Mackensen's decided to call a halt to his offensive. US VI Corps had hung on to its lodgement. Both sides now went over to a strategy of containment. Although his performance in the defensive fighting went some way towards redeeming him, Lucas was replaced as corps commander by MajGen Truscott and returned to the USA.

THE THIRD BATTLE FOR CASSINO

The third battle for Cassino was planned immediately after the second battle had been called off. The feeling in the Allied camp was that pressure had to be maintained on the Gustav Line. With the end of the German offensive on 20 February, the situation at Anzio stabilised and the beachhead was no longer considered particularly vulnerable. General Alexander was also looking at a wider picture and had been briefed by his Chief of Staff, LtGen John Harding, on the need for a major offensive to crack the Gustav Line once and for all. It involved shifting the boundary between US Fifth Army and British Eighth Army to the River Liri and bringing over the Apennines as many of Gen Leese's divisions as possible to make an all-out attack along the whole of the front. Operation Diadem, as it was called, would send four corps containing nine fresh divisions against the Gustav Line between the sea and Cassino to smash their way through the fortified line. Cassino was no longer to be attacked in isolation. Such an operation was extremely complex and could not be undertaken until the fine weather arrived in May. In the meantime the Germans had to be kept occupied.

While Diadem was being planned, Freyberg was told to try again at Cassino. Although it was felt that it was unlikely that a breakthough could be made, if he were to be successful his gains could then act as a springboard for the coming offensive. In his new plan, the commander of II New Zealand Corps decided that he would again attack Cassino town,

LtGen Mark Clark (right) visiting HQ British 5th Division in the Anzio beachhead. In the centre is MajGen Gregson Ellis the divisional commander, with Brig MacLaine Campbell VC, Commander 13th Brigade, on his right. (Imperial War Museum, NA4600)

Polish troops attacking the enemy with grenades. Most of the fighting on the hills around Cassino was at very close quarters with the forward positions on Snakeshead Ridge often only 50 yards apart. (Imperial War Museum, MH1984)

The Allied bombing raid on Cassino prior to the attack by II New Zealand Corps during the third battle. The results were devastating. The whole built up area was reduced to rubble, hindering all movement by supporting armour during Freyberg's attack and leaving perfect defensive positions for the Germans to seize. The raid was supposed to have wiped out the paratroopers holed up in Cassino, and indeed many of them were killed, but even more escaped unscathed to continue with their fanatic defence of the town. (US national Archives)

but this time he would go in from two sides at once, from the north and from the east, supported by tanks. Before these troops were committed, however, the town was to be obliterated by carpet bombing, eliminating the German defenders. At the same time, the 4th Indian Division would attack Monastery Hill, not from Snakeshead Ridge and the positions in the mountains, but along a route just above the town, using an axis from Point 175, Castle Hill, Point 165 and 236, moving up the defile that led to the top of Montecassino from the town. To support the final push against the Abbey, a mixed force of New Zealand and American armour would attempt to get along a road – Cavendish Road – that Engineers were building from Cairo village up past Albaneta Farm. This would put tanks

The results of the bombing of Cassino led to almost insurmountable difficulties for the New Zealand armour trying to support the infantry. Great areas of rubble barred all routes through the town. Attempts by engineers with bulldozers to try to clear routes forward always brought down immediate German retaliatory fire. (Imperial War Museum, NA13800)

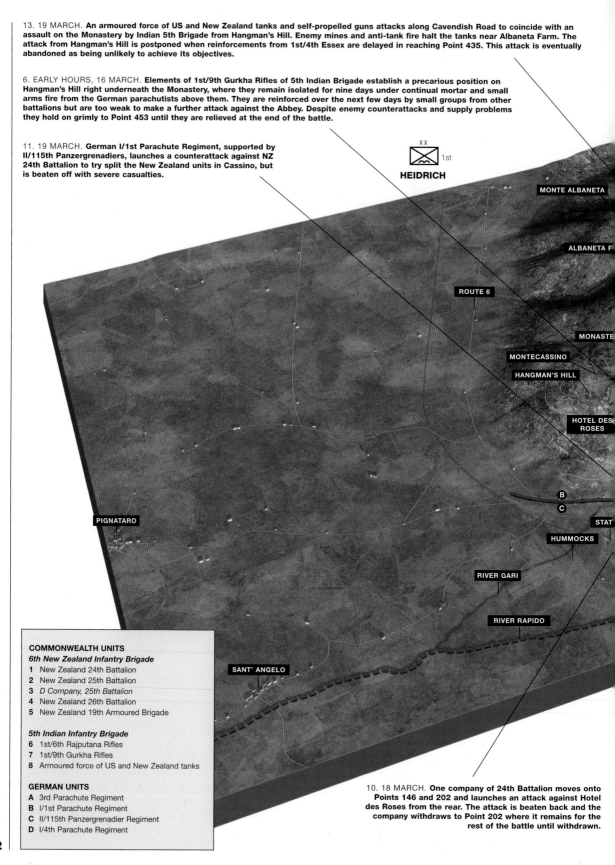

13. 19 MARCH. An armoured force of US and New Zealand tanks and self-propelled guns attacks along Cavendish Road to coincide with an assault on the Monastery by Indian 5th Brigade from Hangman's Hill. Enemy mines and anti-tank fire halt the tanks near Albaneta Farm. The attack from Hangman's Hill is postponed when reinforcements from 1st/4th Essex are delayed in reaching Point 435. This attack is eventually abandoned as being unlikely to achieve its objectives.

6. EARLY HOURS, 16 MARCH. Elements of 1st/9th Gurkha Rifles of 5th Indian Brigade establish a precarious position on Hangman's Hill right underneath the Monastery, where they remain isolated for nine days under continual mortar and small arms fire from the German parachutists above them. They are reinforced over the next few days by small groups from other battalions but are too weak to make a further attack against the Abbey. Despite enemy counterattacks and supply problems they hold on grimly to Point 453 until they are relieved at the end of the battle.

11. 19 MARCH. German I/1st Parachute Regiment, supported by II/115th Panzergrenadiers, launches a counterattack against NZ 24th Battalion to try split the New Zealand units in Cassino, but is beaten off with severe casualties.

XX
1st
HEIDRICH

MONTE ALBANETA

ALBANETA F

ROUTE 6

MONASTE

MONTECASSINO

HANGMAN'S HILL

HOTEL DES ROSES

B
C

PIGNATARO

STAT

HUMMOCKS

RIVER GARI

RIVER RAPIDO

SANT' ANGELO

COMMONWEALTH UNITS
6th New Zealand Infantry Brigade
1 New Zealand 24th Battalion
2 New Zealand 25th Battalion
3 *D Company, 25th Battalion*
4 New Zealand 26th Battalion
5 New Zealand 19th Armoured Brigade

5th Indian Infantry Brigade
6 1st/6th Rajputana Rifles
7 1st/9th Gurkha Rifles
8 Armoured force of US and New Zealand tanks

GERMAN UNITS
A 3rd Parachute Regiment
B I/1st Parachute Regiment
C II/115th Panzergrenadier Regiment
D I/4th Parachute Regiment

10. 18 MARCH. One company of 24th Battalion moves onto Points 146 and 202 and launches an attack against Hotel des Roses from the rear. The attack is beaten back and the company withdraws to Point 202 where it remains for the rest of the battle until withdrawn.

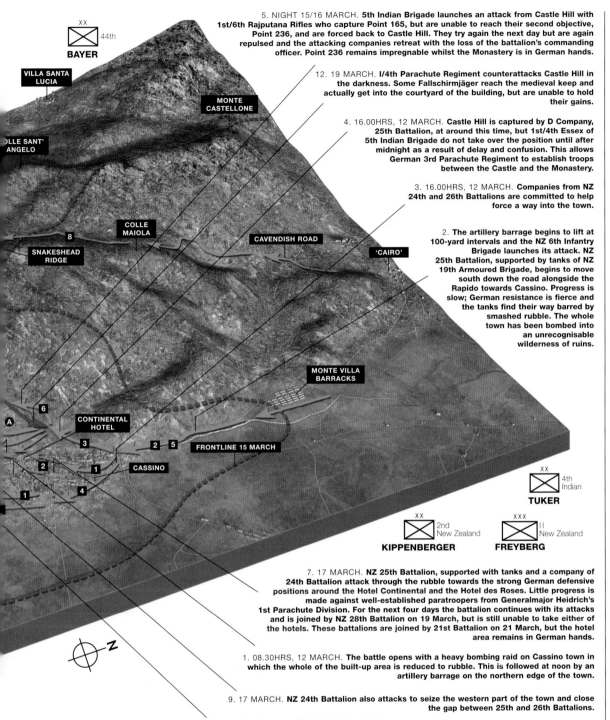

5. NIGHT 15/16 MARCH. **5th Indian Brigade launches an attack from Castle Hill with 1st/6th Rajputana Rifles who capture Point 165, but are unable to reach their second objective, Point 236, and are forced back to Castle Hill. They try again the next day but are again repulsed and the attacking companies retreat with the loss of the battalion's commanding officer. Point 236 remains impregnable whilst the Monastery is in German hands.**

12. 19 MARCH. **I/4th Parachute Regiment counterattacks Castle Hill in the darkness. Some Fallschirmjäger reach the medieval keep and actually get into the courtyard of the building, but are unable to hold their gains.**

4. 16.00HRS, 12 MARCH. **Castle Hill is captured by D Company, 25th Battalion, at around this time, but 1st/4th Essex of 5th Indian Brigade do not take over the position until after midnight as a result of delay and confusion. This allows German 3rd Parachute Regiment to establish troops between the Castle and the Monastery.**

3. 16.00HRS, 12 MARCH. **Companies from NZ 24th and 26th Battalions are committed to help force a way into the town.**

2. **The artillery barrage begins to lift at 100-yard intervals and the NZ 6th Infantry Brigade launches its attack. NZ 25th Battalion, supported by tanks of NZ 19th Armoured Brigade, begins to move south down the road alongside the Rapido towards Cassino. Progress is slow; German resistance is fierce and the tanks find their way barred by smashed rubble. The whole town has been bombed into an unrecognisable wilderness of ruins.**

7. 17 MARCH. **NZ 25th Battalion, supported with tanks and a company of 24th Battalion attack through the rubble towards the strong German defensive positions around the Hotel Continental and the Hotel des Roses. Little progress is made against well-established paratroopers from Generalmajor Heidrich's 1st Parachute Division. For the next four days the battalion continues with its attacks and is joined by NZ 28th Battalion on 19 March, but is still unable to take either of the hotels. These battalions are joined by 21st Battalion on 21 March, but the hotel area remains in German hands.**

1. 08.30HRS, 12 MARCH. **The battle opens with a heavy bombing raid on Cassino town in which the whole of the built-up area is reduced to rubble. This is followed at noon by an artillery barrage on the northern edge of the town.**

9. 17 MARCH. **NZ 24th Battalion also attacks to seize the western part of the town and close the gap between 25th and 26th Battalions.**

8. 17 MARCH. **NZ 26th Battalion, supported by tanks and a company of 24th Battalion, attacks towards the Railway Station. The Station and the Hummocks are captured by a small band of around 100 men and two tanks in the face of heavy opposition. These troops are later reinforced and, despite German counterattacks, the Station remains in Allied hands.**

THE THIRD BATTLE OF CASSINO

12–19 March 1944, viewed from the southeast. New Zealand II Corps' attempt to achieve a breakthrough in the Rapido Valley. They are unable to dislodge the determined German defenders of 1st Parachute Division, despite the controversial bombing of the Monastery and the town of Cassino.

A group of Heidrich's paratroopers in Cassino during the third battle in March. The bombing of the town had destroyed most of the buildings and the German *Fallschirmjäger* turned every cellar and ruined house into a strongpoint. (Bundesarchiv, 146/79/98/9)

behind Point 593 and allow a concerted attack to be made towards the summit of Montecassino and the Monastery.

Generalmajor Baade and his 90th Panzergrenadiers had been rewarded for the brilliant resistance put up around Cassino in the first two battles, by being withdrawn from the sector for a rest and they had been replaced by GenMaj Richard Heidrich and his 1st Parachute Division. These elite troops were no strangers to action and had already fought against the British and Canadians in Sicily and along the Adriatic coast of Italy. There was to be no dilution of the quality of the German troops defending Cassino. General Heidrich now deployed his 3rd Parachute Regiment to occupy the town and Monastery Hill, while 4th Parachute Regiment held the mountains to the north and north-west of Montecassino.

Looking up Montecassino towards the Monastery from Point 165 near to Castle Hill. The rocky outcrop on the left of the skyline is Hangman's Hill, Point 435, which was taken during the Third Battle and held for so long by the isolated group of 1st/9th Gurkhas. (Ken Ford)

The third battle for Cassino began on the 15 March 1944. It had been planned almost a month before, but could not be put into operation until the ground had dried out. Incessant rain had left the whole area waterlogged and Freyberg insisted that three dry days free of any rain would be required before he would launch his operation. Weeks came and went whilst the rain continued. During this time both side harassed each other with shell and mortar fire all along the now static line, punishing the unwary and making life for all the troops utterly miserable.

On 15 March Cassino was bombed by a great fleet of medium bombers from 08.30hrs until 12.00hrs. At midday, an artillery barrage descended on the town and the attack began, with the barrage advancing 100 yards every six minutes. Behind this rolling gunfire came New Zealand 25th Battalion, supported by tanks of the New Zealand 19th Armoured Regiment rolling down the road into Cassino from the north. Almost immediately the plan began to go awry. The bombing and artillery barrage had not eliminated all the German defenders. They had taken heavy casualties, but the survivors sprang from their shelters once the shelling passed and opened up on the New Zealanders with machine-guns. Tanks were of little help, as the bombing had left the roads and streets of the town virtually impassable to armour. Craters pockmarked the route and rubble blocked the thoroughfares. Then it started to rain and the brick dust turned to mud. The 25th Battalion spent the entire afternoon trying to advance just a few hundred yards. 26th Battalion joined the attack just after dark. More men were gradually getting into the town, but their progress forward was slow in the face of determined enemy resistance. The one bright point of success was the capture of Castle Hill at around 16.45hrs.

The medieval strongpoint on its summit was handed over to the men of 1st/4th Essex from 5th Indian Brigade and the remainder of

German paratrooper prisoners being escorted back to the rear from Cassino. Heidrich's paras are moving northwards up the road into Cassino which ran alongside the River Rapido. New Zealand tanks are moving down the road to continue with the attack. Picture taken on 16 March on the second day of LtGen Freyberg's second attempt to take the position. (Imperial War Museum, NA12908)

GERMAN PARATROOPERS DEFENDING CASSINO TOWN FROM THE RUINS OF THE CONTINENTAL HOTEL

(pages 66–68)

Oberst Heilmann's German 3rd Parachute Regiment was deployed in Cassino and around Monastery Hill at the start of the third battle of Cassino. The regiment's II Parachute Battalion, commanded by Major Foltin, supported by 10th Company of the III Parachute Battalion held the town itself. On 15 March 1944 the battle opened with the heavy bombing raid by 600 Allied aircraft, followed by several hours firing by over 750 guns. Not surprisingly, the whole of Cassino was reduced to rubble. Over 220 German paratroopers were buried under its collapsed buildings. Those that survived the bombardment staggered from the debris and set about reinforcing and fortifying the ruins to make each derelict building a strongpoint. They then fought tenaciously to hold on to every square metre of the town. One of the strongest positions was based around the remains of the Continental Hotel, situated on an important road junction where Route 6 winds around the base of Montecassino. A Panzer IV tank was backed into the hotel's reception area and machine guns and mortars emplaced to cover every approach. GenMaj Heidrich's paratroopers held

on to this position throughout the third battle of Cassino and well into the fourth, only giving up the building over two months later when several Allied divisions had got behind them into the Liri valley and the Polish II Corps was above them on Monastery Hill. The scene shows the PzKpfw IV (1) in the ruins of the Continental Hotel sited to fire down Route 6. The New Zealanders found great difficulty attacking through the town and trying to manoeuvre their Shermans through the rubble strewn streets. They lost every tank that attempted to close on the hotel. The German corps commander, GenLt Von Senger und Etterlin, attributes the parachute division's ability to hold the hotel and the western sector of the town to this one tank. Each infantry attack against the position was pinned down by concentrated machine-gun and mortar fire. The paratroopers are manning a MG34 light machine-gun (2), with an NCO (3) acquiring targets through his binoculars. All of them are wearing the second pattern camouflaged jump smock with a silver Luftwaffe eagle on the right breast (4). The Luftwaffe eagle is also prominent on each of their standard Fallschirmjäger helmets (5). The NCO (sergeant) displays his badge of rank as a patch on his collar in the form of two silver wings on a yellow background (6). (Howard Gerrard)

5th Indian Brigade struck out up Monastery Hill through the darkness. Points 165 and 236 were taken and lost by 1st/6th Rajputanas and a small party of 1st/9th Gurkhas made a brilliant night advance and managed to get onto the exposed slopes Hangman's Hill (Point 435) just a few hundred yards below the Abbey, but after a night of fighting little other ground was captured. In the morning, under the cover of smoke, the Rajputanas tried again to get to Point 236. The battalion failed once more with the loss of many men including the commanding officer and the adjutant. Over the next few days, the New Zealanders in the town and the Indian Division in the hills battled away trying to establish themselves securely on key positions.

The Gurkhas on Hangman's Hill were reinforced piecemeal and at great cost. Each man attempting to climb up to the rocky outcrop had to pass across ground criss-crossed with enemy fire. All movement and resupply had to be done under the cover of darkness. The isolated Gurkhas were counterattacked a number of times, but held on tenaciously to their small outpost. In the town, Freyberg fed New Zealand 24th Battalion into the rubble and the three battalions fanned out to take the strategic points. 26th Battalion made it as far as Route 6 and the road was opened to tanks. They could not progress very far, however, for the German paratroopers defending Cassino had tanks and self propelled guns hidden in the bombed out buildings. These took a toll of the armour and the blocked roads and craters made any flanking movements impossible. The New Zealand infantry were made to fight for every street corner, road and pile of rubble.

At daybreak on 17 March, after a night of fighting, the Indian Division managed to put men onto Points 146, 202 and 165, but all were under great pressure from the enemy. In the town 25th Battalion had progressed a little further with the aid of 19th Armoured Regiment's tanks. They managed to get close to the Continental Hotel, but here the move stopped as Heidrich's paratroopers had created a formidable

Cassino was left a scene of devastation after the Allied bombing prior to the start of the third battle. Streets and buildings were obliterated and reduced to piles of rubble. Heidrich's paratroopers took great advantage of this chaos to reinforce and defend every building and locality. (Imperial War Museum, CL4244)

Point 165 on the second hairpin bend on the road up to the Monastery. This viewpoint is with Castle Hill behind us, looking up to Point 445, with Point 236 just out of view to the left. (Ken Ford)

strongpoint around the ruins of this building and the Hotel des Roses and would not be dislodged. New Zealand 26th Battalion pushed as far as the Railway Station assisted by tanks, under attack all the way. Two tanks actually made it to the station and were reinforced by about 100 infantry before night fell. This was a significant success in a day characterised by gains of just a few yards.

By morning on 18 March, the Gurkhas on Hangman's Hill had been resupplied and reinforced as a result of a brave night time sortie by men from 4th/6th Rajputanas. An attempt to attack the Hotel des Roses from the rear from Point 202 had ended in failure, with men from 24th Battalion withdrawing back to their starting point. In the valley, the Railway Station was the target of a vigorous counterattack by the Parachute Machine Gun Battalion, which was broken up with great loss to the enemy. Elsewhere in the town the New Zealanders of 24th and 25th Battalions continued to plug away at the Continental Hotel area trying to make the final push to the south. Little progress was made and the day turned out the same as the previous, with lots of hard fighting, many casualties and virtually no gains. By this time the battle was drifting towards stalemate. The enemy was showing no signs of giving in, quite the opposite for paratroopers actually counterattacked Castle Hill and retook Point 165 in the early hours of 19 March, then penetrated right up the walls of the medieval stronghold before they were beaten back.

General Freyberg was by this time deeply concerned at the lack of progress and decided to launch his final push. He gave orders for the Rajputanas to relieve the 1st/4th Essex on Castle Hill and for the latter to join the Gurkhas on Hangman's Hill. The combined force would then make the final dash for the Monastery. At the same time a force of tanks advancing through the mountains along 'Cavendish Road' would make an attack on the rear.

The Gurkhas were resupplied with ammunition and food was parachuted to them on the afternoon of the 18th. 1st/4th Essex moved up to join them during the night. The reinforcement was dogged by problems as half of the Essex men ran into the counterattack on the Castle and could

Medics work on an injured
New Zealander in the ruins of
Cassino. (Imperial War Museum,
NA13798)

not get forward. By morning they had not arrived on Hangman's Hill and
the attack on the Monastery was postponed until 14.00hrs. Surprisingly, the
armoured advance down Cavendish Road was still launched on schedule
early that morning. It was not a success. The tanks moved out along the
road and achieved a degree of surprise as the Germans had not believed
armour could operate in the mountains. The combined attack by
American and New Zealand tanks passed Phantom Ridge on their left and
got as far as Albaneta Farm just to the rear of Point 565 before its progress
was stopped. It was difficult to deploy the tanks off the road and once one
was knocked out it caused problems for all of the others. More and more
tanks then succumbed to enemy fire in the bottleneck formed and the
attack was called off. Without this armoured thrust, the attack from
Hangman's Hill would have been suicidal and this too was abandoned.

It was a bad day for Freyberg. In the town his fresh 28th Battalion
made no progress at all attacking the Continental Hotel. The rubble-
strewn streets and cratered townscape still made life very difficult for
the armour and the unsupported infantry could not get through the
withering enemy fire. Freyberg now had only two options available;
either call the battle off or reinforce the New Zealand Division for one
last try to capture the town. He chose the latter, but Alexander warned
him that there had to be a quick success or the battle must stop.

On 20 March units from 78th Division relieved elements of the New
Zealand Division. That night Indian 7th Brigade up in the mountains
was told to capture Point 445 to close the ravine between Castle Hill and
Point 175 to the enemy. The 2nd/7th Gurkhas tried as ordered but with

no success; they were unable to cover the last few yards to their objective. In the town, attempts were made to get directly up to Points 146 and 202 to relieve a few detachments that were holding out, but these also failed. The Continental Hotel still remained resolutely in the hands of the German paratroopers, defying numerous attempts to capture it by the now committed 21st New Zealand Battalion. In fact, it was business as usual for both sides: desperately courageous fighting, few gains. It was clear that Gen Heidrich and his Fallschirmjäger had won the third battle of Cassino. On 23 March, Freyberg called his exposed troops down from the outposts on the hills and consolidated his small gains. Part of the town and Castle Hill were made secure and garrisoned by 78th Division, as were the exposed positions of the Indian Division in the hills behind the town. Posts were mined and wire was laid, then the two exhausted divisions of II New Zealand Corps withdrew from Cassino.

A view of Cassino town and Montecassino from the east, taken from a point above Route 6. In the lower foreground, three light bombers fly low over the flooded area of the Rapido Valley spraying insecticide to kill mosquitos and prevent the spread of malaria. (US National Archives)

OPERATION DIADEM: BREAKING THE GUSTAV LINE

New Zealand troops moving through the ruins of Cassino town. The bombing and shelling had reduced most of Cassino to rubble and provided excellent positions for the enemy to defend and difficult ground for the New Zealanders to cover. (Imperial War Museum, NA13284)

Even before the third battle for Cassino was over, units from British Eighth Army were on the move towards the Cassino sector of the Gustav Line. General Alexander's proposed great offensive meant an extensive reorganisation of Fifteenth Army Group. The boundary between Eighth Army and US Fifth Army was shifted southwards and was fixed along the line of the River Liri. General Mark Clark finally relinquished responsibility for the Cassino sector of the Gustav Line and handed it over to the British.

Two months preparation went into Operation Diadem and the last details were fine-tuned during the six weeks that followed the collapse of Freyberg's offensive. Alexander had brought as many divisions as possible from Eighth Army's Adriatic sector, leaving just enough men there to hold the line. Always something of a backwater, the Adriatic sector now became even more marginal as the focus of the Allied effort shifted to Cassino. Other units new to the Italian theatre were now added to those transferred by Alexander, giving him a sledgehammer of a force with which to launch his attack against the German fortified line that had defied him for so long. The bulk of Fifth and Eighth Armies would be concentrated along a 20-mile front between Cassino and the

A Polish 3in. mortar crew firing in support of an attack. Note the ready-to-use field dressing under the netting of the nearest man's helmet. (Imperial War Museum, NA18057)

OPERATION DIADEM – THE ALLIES BREAK THROUGH THE GUSTAV LINE

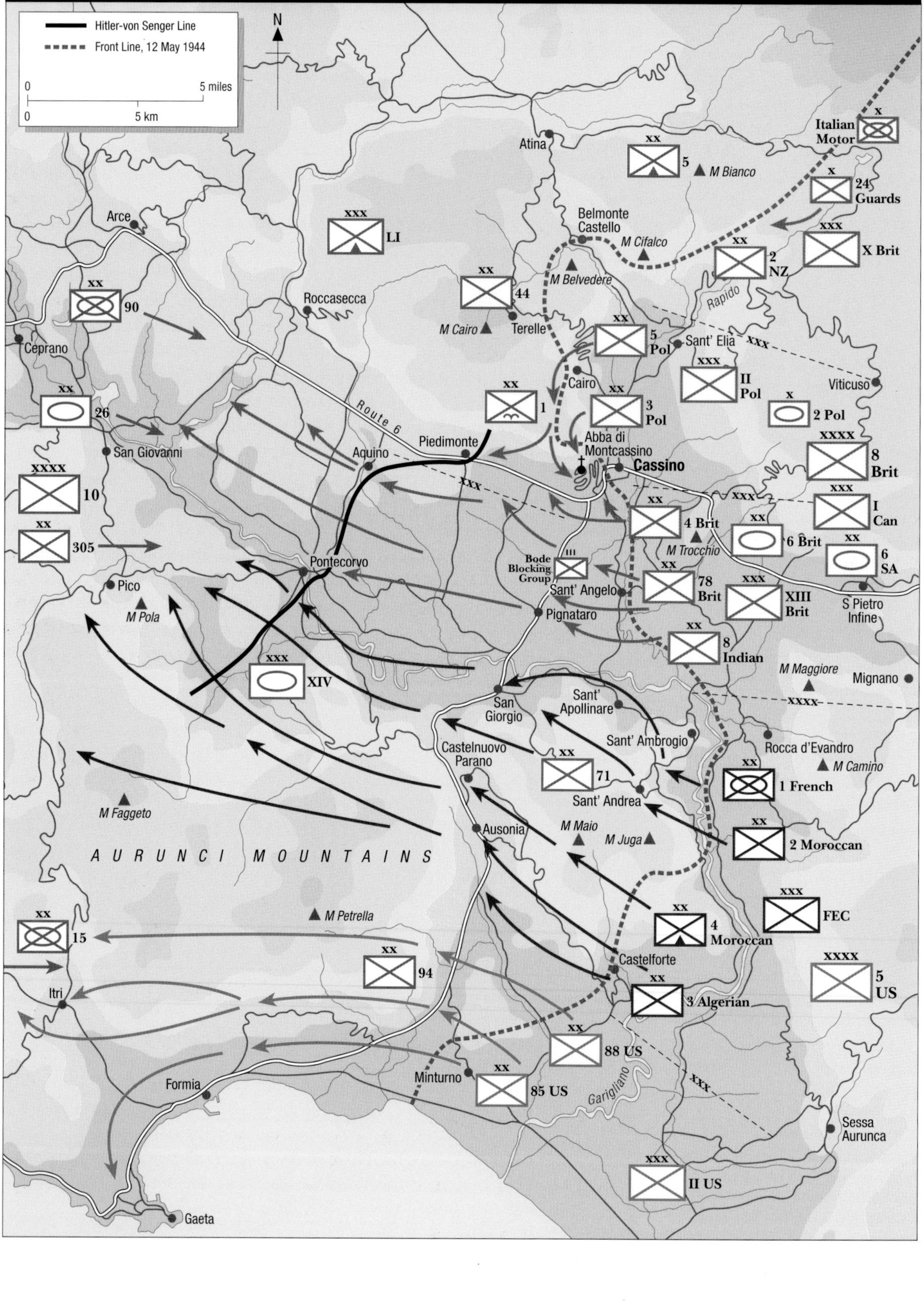

Hitler-von Senger Line

Front Line, 12 May 1944

0   5 miles

0   5 km

N

Atina

M Bianco

5

Arce

Belmonte Castello

M Cifalco

Italian Motor

24 Guards

X Brit

2 NZ

LI

Roccasecca

M Belvedere

44

M Cairo

Terelle

5 Pol

Sant' Elia

II Pol

Viticuso

90

Cairo

1

3 Pol

2 Pol

Ceprano

Route 6

Abba di Montcassino

Cassino

8 Brit

26

Piedimonte

San Giovanni

Aquino

Pontecorvo

4 Brit

M Trocchio

6 Brit

I Can

6 SA

10

Bode Blocking Group

Sant' Angelo

78 Brit

XIII Brit

S Pietro Infine

305

Pico

M Pola

Pignataro

8 Indian

M Maggiore

Mignano

XIV

San Giorgio

Sant' Apollinare

Sant' Ambrogio

Rocca d'Evandro

M Camino

M Faggeto

Castelnuovo Parano

Sant' Andrea

M Maio

71

1 French

2 Moroccan

A U R U N C I   M O U N T A I N S

Ausonia

M Juga

15

M Petrella

94

Castelforte

4 Moroccan

FEC

Itri

3 Algerian

5 US

Formia

Minturno

85 US

88 US

Gariglano

Sessa Aurunca

Gaeta

II US

74

Gurkhas from 1st/5th Gurkha Rifles of 8th Indian Division, smartly turned out for the camera before going into action during the final battle to break the Gustav Line. (Imperial War Museum)

sea, ready to smash a way through German Tenth Army. They would have superiority in infantry, artillery and armour and would be able to call upon the overwhelming might of the Allied air forces. Key to success was the rapidity of the initial thrust, which would deny the enemy the opportunity to fall back and occupy the new defensive line they had built six miles behind the Gustav Line – the Hitler Line [2].

The first units to arrive were the two divisions and armour of Polish II Corps and they went into the line above Cassino to take over the positions held by British 78th Division. The corps' commander, Lieutenant-General Wladyslaw Anders, was now given responsibility for containing the enemy in this sector and for the final capture of Montecassino. His two infantry divisions, 3rd Carpathian Division and 5th Kresowa Division, had Polish 2nd Armoured Brigade in support.

In preparation for Diadem, Alexander lined up his two armies along the start line. Closest to the sea was US Fifth Army's II Corps, now composed of two completely new divisions, US 85th and 88th Divisions. Their task in the operation was to drive up the axis of Route 7 and link up with US VI Corps at Anzio. On US II Corps' right was Gen Juin's French Expeditionary Corps, transferred from the mountains to the far side of the sector on the lower Garigliano. It had been expanded from two to four divisions with the arrival of 1st French Motorised Division and 4th Moroccan Mountain Division. General Juin's four divisions would attack through the Aurunci Mountains and then wheel to the right to sweep down into the Liri valley behind the Gustav Line.

To Juin's right, along the line of the Rapido, was British XIII Corps with 4th British Division and 8th Indian Division. These two divisions would make the initial assault across the river either side of Sant' Angelo, while 78th Division and British 6th Armoured Division waited in the rear, ready to exploit their bridgehead. In support, poised to continue the momentum once a breakthrough had been achieved, was Canadian I Corps with its 1st Infantry Division and 5th Armoured Division. These six divisions would deliver the weight of the attack, with the object of smashing through the Gustav Line and then onto the Hitler (von Senger) Line before it could be manned. The way would then be open to Rome.

On the right of LtGen Sidney Kirkman's XIII Corps was LtGen Anders Polish II Corps in the mountains above Cassino while the 1st Guards Brigade held the line through Cassino town itself. In the mountains to the right of the Poles, in the sector the French had contested for so long, was British X Corps; New Zealand II Corps had been disbanded at the end of March.

US VI Corps at Anzio, by this time reinforced and resupplied, was ready to break out of its beachhead once the offensive got underway. Truscott's corps had received US 34th and 36th Divisions from II Corps

---

2 Also known as the von Senger Line.

and also British 5th Division to strengthen its garrison. British 56th Division had been withdrawn to Egypt for a refit. Alexander's plan was for VI Corps to strike out of its lodgement at the appropriate moment and make for Valmontone on Route 6 to cut off the retreating German Tenth Army. Operation Diadem would begin some days before VI Corps launched its own breakout. General Alexander would judge the right moment, probably around four days after Diadem began.

There had also been some reorganisation on the German side, with the River Liri also marking a corps boundary – in this case between von Senger's XIV Panzer Corps and Gen Valin Feurstein's LI Mountain Corps. XIV Panzer Corps thus faced the French and Americans of US Fifth Army while LI Mountain Corps confronted the British and Poles of Eighth Army. On the left wing of Gen Feurstein's corps holding the northerly mountainous region was 5th Mountain Division, with 44th Division to its right. At the start of Operation Diadem, 5th Mountain Division was in the process of extending its front southwards and pinching out 44th Division so that it could be withdrawn from the line. This happened just at the moment that the Poles attacked causing the enemy great confusion.

Major General B.M. Hoffmeister, Commander 5th Canadian Armoured Division, in his Sherman tank 'Vancouver' moving through the Liri Valley during Operation Diadem. (Strathy Smith/National Archives of Canada/PA-201346)

Still holding the Cassino sector itself was Heidrich's 1st Parachute Division. In the Liri valley, ensconced in the main fortifications of the Gustav Line was a collection of units from various divisions including the 115th Regiment of 15th Panzergrenadier Division, two battalions of infantry from 305th Infantry Division and the Parachute Machine Gun Battalion of Heidrich's division. This was known as Kampfgruppe Bode, or the Bode Blocking Group. Between the Liri and the sea, von Senger had just two divisions holding the peaks of the Aurunci Mountains: 71st Division on the left opposite the French and 94th Division on the right facing the Americans.

Generalfeldmarschal Kesselring knew that the Allies were massing for an offensive against the Gustav Line, but did not know where or when the blow would fall. He also expected another Allied landing in his rear and felt sure that a seaborne assault would take place near Civitavecchia, or even further north in the region of La Spezia–Leghorn. This fear was reinforced when intelligence told him that the Allies were undertaking amphibious exercises in the Bay of Naples. To counter these landings he had to hold his mobile divisions in reserve ready to move. His Army Group reserves, the 92nd Infantry Division and the *Hermann Göring* Fallschirm Panzer Division were kept north of Rome, with Tenth Army's reserves, the 26th and the 29th Panzergrenadiers, stationed close to the Anzio sector. Baade's rested 90th Panzergrenadiers were at Frosinone within easy striking distance of both the Gustav Line and Anzio.

Alexander launched his offensive with a massive artillery barrage by 1,060 guns at 23.00hrs on 11 May. All along the front battalions of heavy, medium and field guns zeroed in on known and suspected enemy strongpoints. For 40 minutes the guns concentrated on these German positions before switching to bombard the Allied infantry's first objectives. The Americans moved off on the left in the early hours of 12 May following behind the barrage, with 85th Division thrusting along the coast and the

MajGen Keightley (right), Commander British 78th 'Battleaxe' Division, and two of his staff study a topographical model of the terrain around Montecassino. Keightley's division took over responsibility for part of Cassino town and the area of Snakeshead Ridge from the Indian and New Zealand Divisions after the end of the third battle. His infantry remained holding the static front line until just before the start of Operation Diadem in May when they relinquished it to Anders' Polish corps. (Imperial War Museum, NA13591)

88th Division keeping step with the 3rd Algerian Division alongside them. The Americans made only slow progress to begin with against a well-established German 94th Division. Support came from the guns of warships out at sea and from US fighter-bombers. For three days progress was steady, but not spectacular, then on 14 May Generalleutnant Steinmetz's 94th Division began to fall back, forced to leave its prepared positions under pressure from the Americans and, more specifically, from the French.

General Juin's corps made excellent early progress. His fearless North Africans were up in the mountains and amongst the enemy's 71st Division as fast as they were able, achieving startling results in the first two days. Monte Maio, the southern pillar of the entrance to the Liri valley opposite Montecassino, fell to the 4th Moroccan Division on 13 May and Juin's men advanced north-west to look down into the Liri valley that evening. The 2nd Moroccan and 3rd Algerian Division swept past Castelforte and up into the mountains moving westwards parallel to the Liri valley. Behind them, the French 1st Motorised Division waited to be introduced into the battle.

Along the centre of the line, opposite the entrance of the Liri valley, Kirkman's XIII Corps began its battle. On the left, next to the French was 8th Indian Division and it made its assault across the Rapido downstream of Sant' Angelo. Enemy resistance was just as fierce as that which had greeted Walker's Texas Division when it had attempted the same feat four months previously, but Allied firepower was now greater and the weight of the attack much heavier. The Indians managed to get bridges and a few tanks across during the first 24 hours and were strong enough to withstand numerous counterattacks. Gradually a lodgement was made and it slowly enlarged as more troops and armour were fed into the bridgehead. Up river of Sant' Angelo was the crossing place of British 4th Division. It fared less well and was unable to bridge the river until the morning of 14 May. This crossing was the closest to Cassino and suffered as a result of the excellent observation that the Germans had of the crossing site. Every time a bridgehead looked to have been won it was counterattacked. Vietinghoff had by this time sent his reserves into the Liri valley and resistance was intense. British 4th Division's crossing place was close to Route 6 and the enemy was determined to keep the use of this road from the Allies.

THE FOURTH BATTLE OF CASSINO

Up in the mountains around Montecassino, Gen Anders' Polish Corps made its move, just as the other Allied assaults were going in. In the darkness of the early hours of 12 May, Anders attacked with his two infantry divisions. His plan was not to use his men in 'penny packets' as had been done in all the other attempts, where an attack on one strongpoint drew

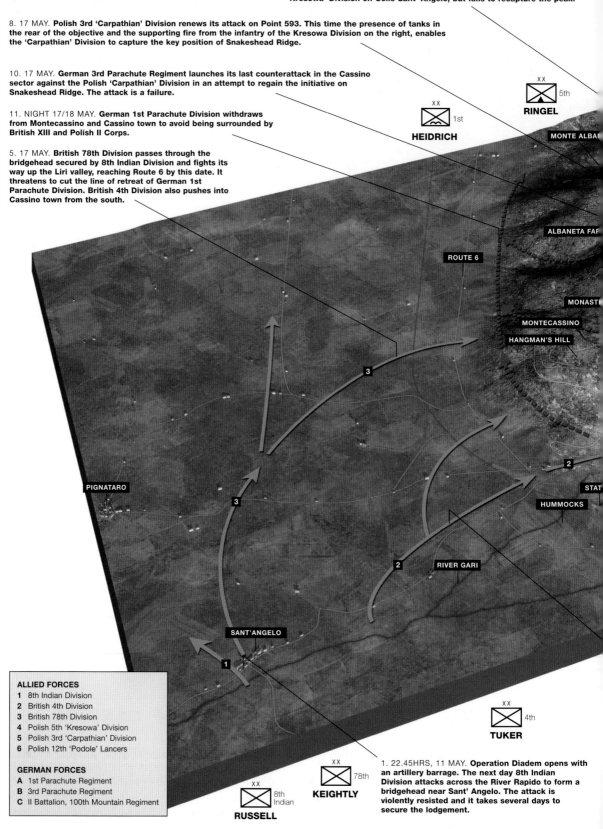

9. 17 MAY. **II Battalion, German 100th Mountain Regiment counterattacks the 'Kresowa' Division on Colle Sant' Angelo, but fails to recapture the peak.**

8. 17 MAY. **Polish 3rd 'Carpathian' Division renews its attack on Point 593. This time the presence of tanks in the rear of the objective and the supporting fire from the infantry of the Kresowa Division on the right, enables the 'Carpathian' Division to capture the key position of Snakeshead Ridge.**

10. 17 MAY. **German 3rd Parachute Regiment launches its last counterattack in the Cassino sector against the Polish 'Carpathian' Division in an attempt to regain the initiative on Snakeshead Ridge. The attack is a failure.**

11. NIGHT 17/18 MAY. **German 1st Parachute Division withdraws from Montecassino and Cassino town to avoid being surrounded by British XIII and Polish II Corps.**

5. 17 MAY. **British 78th Division passes through the bridgehead secured by 8th Indian Division and fights its way up the Liri valley, reaching Route 6 by this date. It threatens to cut the line of retreat of German 1st Parachute Division. British 4th Division also pushes into Cassino town from the south.**

RINGEL
xx 5th

MONTE ALBA

HEIDRICH
xx 1st

MONTE ALBAN

ALBANETA FAR

ROUTE 6

MONAST

MONTECASSINO

HANGMAN'S HILL

3

PIGNATARO

3

2

STAT

HUMMOCKS

2   RIVER GARI

SANT'ANGELO

1

ALLIED FORCES
1 8th Indian Division
2 British 4th Division
3 British 78th Division
4 Polish 5th 'Kresowa' Division
5 Polish 3rd 'Carpathian' Division
6 Polish 12th 'Podole' Lancers

GERMAN FORCES
A 1st Parachute Regiment
B 3rd Parachute Regiment
C II Battalion, 100th Mountain Regiment

TUKER
xx 4th

78th
KEIGHTLY

8th
Indian
RUSSELL

1. 22.45HRS, 11 MAY. **Operation Diadem opens with an artillery barrage. The next day 8th Indian Division attacks across the River Rapido to form a bridgehead near Sant' Angelo. The attack is violently resisted and it takes several days to secure the lodgement.**

78

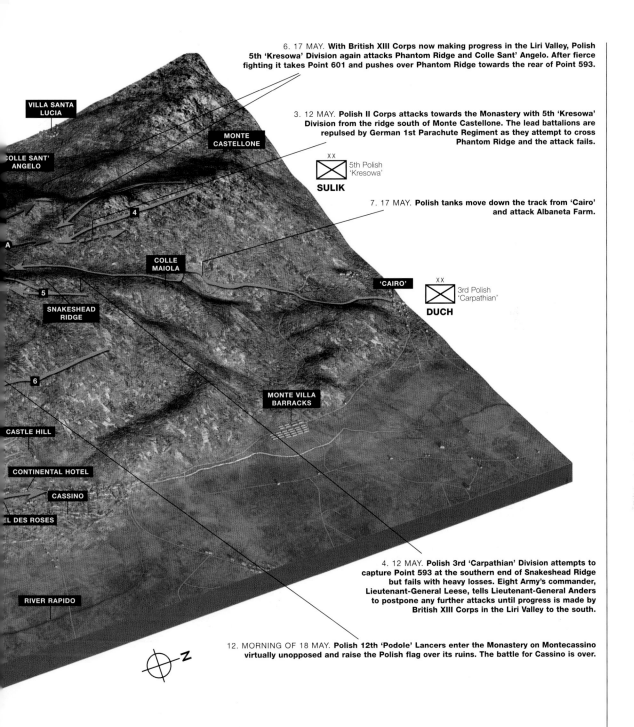

6. 17 MAY. With British XIII Corps now making progress in the Liri Valley, Polish 5th 'Kresowa' Division again attacks Phantom Ridge and Colle Sant' Angelo. After fierce fighting it takes Point 601 and pushes over Phantom Ridge towards the rear of Point 593.

3. 12 MAY. Polish II Corps attacks towards the Monastery with 5th 'Kresowa' Division from the ridge south of Monte Castellone. The lead battalions are repulsed by German 1st Parachute Regiment as they attempt to cross Phantom Ridge and the attack fails.

XX
5th Polish 'Kresowa'

SULIK

7. 17 MAY. Polish tanks move down the track from 'Cairo' and attack Albaneta Farm.

XX
3rd Polish 'Carpathian'

'CAIRO'

DUCH

VILLA SANTA LUCIA

MONTE CASTELLONE

COLLE SANT' ANGELO

4

A

COLLE MAIOLA

5

SNAKESHEAD RIDGE

6

MONTE VILLA BARRACKS

CASTLE HILL

CONTINENTAL HOTEL

CASSINO

EL DES ROSES

RIVER RAPIDO

4. 12 MAY. Polish 3rd 'Carpathian' Division attempts to capture Point 593 at the southern end of Snakeshead Ridge but fails with heavy losses. Eight Army's commander, Lieutenant-General Leese, tells Lieutenant-General Anders to postpone any further attacks until progress is made by British XIII Corps in the Liri Valley to the south.

12. MORNING OF 18 MAY. Polish 12th 'Podole' Lancers enter the Monastery on Montecassino virtually unopposed and raise the Polish flag over its ruins. The battle for Cassino is over.

⊕ Z

2. 12 MAY. British 4th Division attacks across the Rapido and after heavy fighting secures a bridgehead. The division then turns north to clear the southern end of Cassino town.

POLISH II CORPS CAPTURES THE MONASTERY

11–18 May 1944, viewed from the southeast. As part of General Alexander's blockbuster offensive to break through the Gustav Line (Operation Diadem), Lieutenant-General Anders' Polish II Corps is given the task of finally eliminating German resistance and capturing the Monastery.

German Panther tank knocked out by Canadian 5th Armoured Division in the Liri Valley. (Alexander M. Stirton/Canada Dept. Of National Defence/National Archives of Canada/ PA-130354)

fire from adjacent positions, but to attack as many of them as he could simultaneously. He pushed down Snakeshead Ridge with 3rd Carpathian Division and along Phantom Ridge with the 5th Kresowa Division, attempting to seize the notorious positions of Points 593, 569, 444 and Albaneta Farm with the Carpathians and Colle Sant Angelo, Points 601, 575 and 505 with the men of the Kresowa Division. In reply, Heidrich's famed paratroopers dealt with the Poles in the same way as they had dealt with all other attempts to dislodge them. They poured down a deluge of fire on the exposed infantrymen inflicting murderous casualties as they tried to move out across the open rock strewn landscape. The German fire had lost none of its venom in the weeks since the Indians had tried the same tactics. Bravery alone could not get Anders' men forward, for nothing could silence the German defenders. Throughout the night the

GenMaj Richard Heidrich, Commander 1st Parachute Division (left), GenFM Wolfram Richthofen, Commander Luftwaffe 2nd Air Fleet (centre) and GenLt Valin Feurstein, Commander LI Mountain Corps (right). (Imperial War Museum, HU55132)

British soldier standing near the graves of two Germans, buried beneath the ruins of the Monastery on Montecassino. (Imperial War Museum, TAP 24288)

Poles battered away with great energy and determination, some new ground on Phantom Ridge was taken and point 593 was seized, but once daylight came enemy snipers and mortar fire picked off the defenders of these exposed positions and whittled away at their strength. By the afternoon, it was clear to Anders that these gains were untenable, the positions could not be reinforced or resupplied. He gave orders for the men to return to their start line; nothing had been gained in the attack.

Lieutenant-General Leese came forward to visit Anders that day and commiserated with the Polish general, accepting some blame for allowing the Poles to attack too soon. He told Anders that his men would have another chance to seize the Monastery, but they would only be unleashed when Eighth Army had got XIII Corps into the Liri Valley behind Montecassino. He told the corps commander to consolidate his positions and prepare for the next battle in which Cassino would finally fall.

After the French had captured Monte Maio the German 71st Infantry Division started to disintegrate. A number of gaps began opening in its line and the Algerians and Moroccans moved at ease over the slopes of the mountains. Units of *goumiers* in their drab-striped gowns traversed impossible ground, outflanking and outmanoeuvring enemy positions. Isolated pockets of Germans were eliminated with ruthless determination. Juin now introduced his 1st Motorised Division and its advanced units filtered down the slopes of the Aurunci Mountains into the Liri valley, moving alongside 8th Indian Division.

Nearer the sea the Americans exploited the enemy's misfortunes and took advantage of slackening of the defence achieved by the success of the French corps. Both 85th and 88th Division slowly pushed back German 94th Division who saw the gap on its left flank widening alarmingly. This whole southern sector of the Gustav Line teetered close to collapse. When it broke the French would sweep into the Liri valley and the Americans up along Route 7 to Anzio. By the fourth day of the battle, it was at breaking point.

LtGen Oliver Leese, Commander British Eight Army (right) in discussion with MajGen Burns, Commander Canadian I Corps (centre), during Operation Diadem. (Imperial War Museum, NA10987)

**POLISH INFANTRY FROM THE 3RD CARPATHIAN DIVISION
FIGHTING ALONG SNAKESHEAD RIDGE TOWARDS
POINT 593 DURING THE FOURTH BATTLE FOR CASSINO,
12 MAY 1944** (pages 82–83)

The ruined Monastery (1) on top of Montecassino dominated
the battlefield around Cassino. It looked down on both the
approaches to the town (2) and into the Liri valley (3), up
which the Allies must pass. The other side of the valley was
anchored by the enemy-held Aurunci Mountains (4) that also
overlooked Route 6, the road to Rome. Some observation of
the enemy was possible from the Allied-held Monte Trocchio
(5), but its lesser height did not allow it to dominate any part
of the battlefield. The Polish attack along Snakeshead Ridge
during the fourth operation to take Montecassino was the
culmination of all the battles that had taken place before on
the heights behind the Monastery. The Germans had held
onto the barren knoll at the southern end of Snakeshead
Ridge (Point 593) since the American 34th Division attacked
them in January. The carefully defended position on a bare
outcrop of rock could only be taken by hand-to-hand
fighting and every attempt during the previous four months
by various divisions of US Fifth Army had failed. The lines
were so close together that Artillery fire and mortars could
not be effectively used. Each German had to be winkled out
of his stone redoubt by physical force. At the start of the
battle Polish 3rd Carpathian Division held the northern end
of the ridge, but the enemy had stubbornly resisted all
attempts to evict them from the Point 593. The ridge was
overlooked by the enemy from the west and subjected to
intense artillery and mortar fire by them. To the east, the

German paratroops in the ruined Monastery on top of
Montecassino had a perfect line of sight to the ridge,
making all movement difficult. The hills surrounding the
Monastery were covered with sparse vegetation, mostly
scrub, grassy outcrops and small trees. The ground was
strewn with boulders and rocks with little subsoil, which
made the digging of defensive positions nigh on impossible.
Shelter had to be made from stacking rocks together,
rather than excavating holes in the ground. The German
emplacement that the Polish infantry are attacking (6) is no
more than a pile of rocks, stones and boulders, supported
with sandbags. Its low profile makes it almost invisible in
the boulder-strewn landscape. The Germans defending it
are well hidden; nothing can be seen of them. The Polish
troops from the 3rd Carpathian Division are all wearing
standard British battledress and carrying British weapons
and equipment (7). The division had been formed in
Palestine in May 1942 from the independent Carpathian
Rifle Brigade, which had been raised in 1940 by Polish
exiles who had escaped to the west in 1939/40. Its numbers
were swelled by men who had been prisoners of war in
Russia after the fall of Poland. Their release from the USSR
was negotiated in August 1942 and Gen Anders led them
out of Russia to the Middle East via Iraq. The division was
equipped, trained and organized according to British
practice and joined British Eighth Army in Italy in late
1943. The divisional badge was a green fir tree on a divided
white and red background (8), the fir tree representing the
forest-covered Carpathian Mountains of southern Poland.
(Howard Gerrard)

Polish infantry resting in the ruined catacombs of the Monastery after its capture. (Imperial War Museum, NA15143)

On British Eighth Army's front a slow, ponderous battle was being fought. Pitted against it were the bulk of the German reserves and the strongest of the enemy's defences. The Liri valley was still the key to the battle and the road to Rome, but if the French continued with their flanking movement, they might be able to engineer their own break-through. On 15 May, Kirkman introduced his 78th Division into the battle, pushing it into 4th Division's bridgehead and supporting it with the tanks of British 6th Armoured Division. There now began a battle of attrition for command of the valley. The 78th Division slogged away at the defenders and pounded the defences. Slowly the enemy began to give way, all the while keeping a tight control on events so as to be able to withdraw behind the fortifications of the Hitler Line.

British 4th Division now wheeled to the right and cut Route 6 to the rear of Montecassino. They continued down the road into Cassino town itself, pushing right into the shattered streets and linking up with the Guards Brigade in and around the Railway Station. On 16 May, 78th Division advanced past the southern base of Montecassino and for the first time put Allied troops beyond Monastery Hill. It was now time to unleash II Polish Corps once more.

General Anders attacked at 18.00hrs on 16 May. Once again he committed both of his divisions, but with slight intervals between their assaults. Two battalions of 5th Kresowa Division swept along Phantom Ridge and by early next morning had captured the whole spine of high ground then continued the advance towards Colle Sant Angelo. Enemy resistance from Heidrich's men was still strong, but events down on the valley floor were beginning to render their hold on the area very precarious. Early on 17 May, Anders released his 3rd Carpathian Division

A German paratrooper looking across the Liri valley from the southern slopes of Montecassino. This was the ground over which the assault divisions of British 8th Army had to fight their way forward during Operation Diadem. Every square metre of the battlefield was under observation by the enemy, until Polish II Corps dislodged Heidrich's men from the commanding heights. (Bundesarchiv, 146/74/6/62)

along Snakeshead Ridge. Just as before, progress was difficult and costly, but little by little the Poles began to take ground. In the early afternoon, Polish armour began to move down Cavendish Road and attacked Albeneta Farm. Fighting continued to be ferocious, but by first light the next morning the farm had fallen to the Poles. A little later Colle Sant Angelo was also captured. The climax of the battle was now close and Gen Anders threw everything he had into the attack. He felt that victory was within his grasp, and indeed it proved to be so, for during the night Heidrich ordered his men to begin an orderly withdrawal from the mountains and to fall back into the defences of the Hitler Line.

With the dominating heights now in their possession, the 3rd Carpathian Division fought their way across the few hundred yards up to the Monastery, over ground that had proved beyond the reach of so many men of so many different nationalities. With Allied troops in front, behind and on their flank, the German defenders in the Monastery melted away. At 10.20hrs on 18 May, men of the 12th Podolski Lancers entered the ruined Abbey and planted the red and white Polish Flag over its battered ruins. Montecassino had fallen.

On the flanks of Alexander's forces, Cassino and Montecassino had been captured, the French were through the Mountains on the left and the Americans were driving up Route 7. In the centre the slogging match went on. General Leese now introduced I Canadian Corps into the battle through 8th Indian Division's bridgehead, sending it forward to break the Hitler Line. Leese told Alexander that he was ready to make his attack on the new German defensive line on the night of 21/22 May. The commander of Fifteenth Army Group now decided that it was time for Truscott's VI Corps to break out of the Anzio perimeter. He gave orders to Gen Clark for the offensive to be directed against Valmontone in order to cut off the retreat of Vietinghoff's Tenth Army up Route 6.

The battle to break out from the Anzio lodgement began on 23 May with US 3rd Division, US 1st Armoured Division and the Special Service Force attacking towards Cisterna against the German 362nd and 715th Infantry Divisions. After two days of fighting a breach was made in the

A group of Canadian infantry examining the remains of an 'Ostwallturm' on the Hitler Line defences. The Ostwallturm was a specially designed fixed fortification based on the PzKpfw V Panther turret, although some normal Panther turrets were dug in along the Hitler Line. (Strathy Smith/National Archives of Canada/PA-114913)

British troops advancing over the River Melfa northwest of the Hitler Line in May 1944 during Operation Diadem. (Imperial War Museum, NA15519)

German lines and 36th Division pushed through, shortly afterwards meeting up with US II Corps who had driven up against negligible resistance along the coast from the Garigliano. General Clark's two forces, separated since mid-January, were at last reunited. Alexander's timing of the breakout was perfect; Tenth Army was facing defeat and Fourteenth Army had little armoured support in the area to prevent it.

Back in the Liri valley the fight continued. The attack on the Hitler Line had begun slightly earlier than planned when Juin's French corps arrived at the southern end as it reached Pico. The French divisions then turned northwards and began to roll up the enemy positions. In the centre the advance of Eighth Army up to the German fortifications was quicker than the enemy had expected and many of the positions were not garrisoned. The chaotic nature of Tenth Army's withdrawal had left too little time for the line to be fully established. The guns and mortars that were to form much of its firepower lay strewn across the battlefield. A great deal of costly fighting was still needed to break the Hitler Line, but the weight of the British and Canadian attack saw the line crumble in just two days, sending those elements of Tenth Army that could extract themselves reeling back. The way to Rome was now open.

THE DRIVE ON ROME

Kesselring fully appreciated the implications of the Allied breakout from Anzio and the threat that US VI Corps would seize Valmontone on Route 6, cutting off German Tenth Army, but there was little he could

A German 75mm PAK 40 antitank gun knocked out by British Eighth Army during the advance through the Liri valley. (Alexander M. Stirton/Canada Dept. Of National Defence/National Archives of Canada/Pa-189925)

do. Events were happening too fast and there were no more reserves to throw into the battle. The Field Marshal had been outmanoeuvred and out-fought by Alexander who now had the opportunity that he had been waiting for since January when the Anzio landings were first proposed. The main object of those landings and of Operation Diadem was not just to seize ground, but to cut off and destroy German Tenth Army. Rome would then inevitably fall and the whole of Italy up to the great mountain ranges in the north would be open to the Allies.

In the Liri valley fighting remained intense, but the Germans were all the while trying to evacuate the Hitler Line and withdraw towards Rome. It was not a rout, for rearguard actions, mined roads and booby-trapped obstacles slowed the pursuit and prevented the Allies from catching the main body of troops. Massive traffic jams also added to Eighth Army's problems as three armoured divisions – South African 6th Armoured Division had also been introduced into the battle – and several independent armoured formations joined in the pursuit. Lorried infantry added to the tailbacks on the few metalled roads.

On the Anzio front events took a sudden turn that astounded both Allied and German High Commands. Late on 25 May, General Clark changed the orders given to him by his boss General Alexander and switched the weight of his attack. He told Truscott to continue the drive towards Valmontone with just one division, the now exhausted 3rd Division, while the remainder of his corps were to swing to the left along Route 7 heading for the Alban Hills and Rome. Four divisions, the 34th, 36th, 45th and 1st Armored Divisions now mounted a concentrated thrust for the capital. British 1st and 5th Division were given the task of holding the left flank.

US 3rd Division got to within three miles of Valmontone before it was completely halted by a battle group made up of elements of 334th, 92nd and *Hermann Göring* Divisions. This combined enemy force held Route 6 open allowing the bulk of Vietinghoff's retreating Tenth Army to pass through. Almost before their eyes, the Americans watched the Germans escape from the trap that had been planned for so long. Meanwhile Clark's drive on Rome ran into some resistance from a hastily created defence line known as the Caesar Line. For four days US VI Corps, strengthened by the arrival of II Corps, pounded away at the line. When it finally broke on 4 June, the Americans rushed into Rome with Clark at their head. The commander of US Fifth Army had seized the prize he so badly wanted and became the liberator of the Holy City, but at great cost to his military reputation.

Kesselring and Vietinghoff could not believe their luck when Clark changed the direction of VI Corps' advance and failed to slam the door on Tenth Army at Valmontone. Their surprise was matched by that within Allied command. Even Clark's own corps commander, MajGen Truscott, was 'dumbfounded' by the action. Clark had been suspicious of British motives and was determined that US Fifth Army would seize Rome and the glory that went with it.

Other formations were now approaching Rome. Juin's corps skirted round the eastern side of the city and Leese's army cut across the

Canadian troops examine a knocked out German Panther tank along the Hitler Line in May 1944. (Strathy Smith/National Archives of Canada/PA-115778)

hills and continued to pursue the enemy up the east bank of the River Tiber. Clark's army was bogged down clearing the city, choked by ever increasing traffic congestion. Kesselring's forces, meanwhile, continued their orderly and controlled retreat up the spine of Italy.

The battle for Italy continued for a further 11 months. Alexander's task did not get any easier. The Germans continued to fight their rearguard actions on several river and mountain lines, withdrawing into the Gothic Line in the mountains in the north. The line was similar in many ways to the Gustav Line. It had been prepared well in advance and once again consisted of well-sited strongpoints in the mountains, fixed concrete defences and interlocking fields of artillery, machine gun and mortar fire. By the time Fifteenth Army Group had reached the line it was winter once more and its men had to contend with their old enemies wind, rain, sleet and snow. Alexander's forces had also been depleted in the summer when he had been ordered to hand over some of his best divisions to take part in the landings in southern France in August.

Before the end came in Italy, changes in command were made. Alexander took over from Wilson as Supreme Commander Mediterranean, with Clark becoming head of Fifteenth Army Group. Truscott relieved him as Commander US Fifth Army and McCreery took over Eighth Army from Leese. In the spring of 1945 Clark fought a great offensive to breach the Gothic Line and the defences along the River Po that led to the total collapse of German forces in Italy. On 2 May, Vietinghoff, who had taken over command of the theatre from Kesselring a month before, surrendered to Clark bringing the war in Italy to an end.

THE BATTLEFIELD TODAY

Today's visitor to the Gustav Line will have to look hard to find any sign of the German fortified positions. Much of the land has returned to its agricultural roots and is once more back in the care of its farmers and gardeners. The Liri valley presents a pastoral scene where 60 years ago men fought for their lives. But one thing has not changed and would be instantly recognised by any of the veterans of the conflict who returned to the area: Montecassino and its Monastery still looks down on every corner of the old battlefield, towering above the flat lands, watching every movement in the valley below.

Cassino lies two miles to the north of the motorway that sweeps traffic down from Rome through the Liri valley and on to the holiday delights of Naples and Sorrento. The town of Cassino has been completely rebuilt and revitalised since its destruction, as not one building survived the bombing and shelling of 1944. Cassino is a remarkably ugly modern town, it has little to commend it except for the frenzied energy with which it continues to carry out its business affairs. The ancient highway of Route 6, now clogged with local traffic, still passes through the town along its old path, turning sharply to the left at the site of the Continental Hotel. A little further on the right, by the site of the Hotel des Roses, is the start of the road that snakes its way through numerous hairpin bends up to the Abbey.

The Benedictine Abbey on Montecassino, which was completely destroyed during the fighting, has been rebuilt exactly as it was, returned to its pre-war condition by the restoration of its many treasures, saved by

The German War Cemetery on a hillside overlooking Cairo village to the north of Cassino. In the background, the cleft in the hills marks the start of the route up to the hills surrounding Montecassino. All troops, supplies, equipment and ammunition had to pass up this valley, carried forward by hand or on mules. (Ken Ford)

the Germans before the battle. It is now the main attraction for visitors to Cassino, for the Abbey welcomes tourists through its massive portals into the area where so many of Gen Heidrich's paratroopers fought and died. In the crypt, St Benedict's tomb remains intact, despite being hit by a shell that pierced its fabric and did not explode.

The twisting route up to the Monastery winds its way through the exposed rock strewn hillside that was once so deadly to cross. At the second hairpin is the gentle sloping track leading up to the Castle. This bend is just to the east of Point 165, which the Rajputanas tried to capture many times, only to be thrown back at each attempt. The Castle has been closed to the public for a considerable time for refurbishment, but will no doubt soon reopen so that the military enthusiast, and medieval scholar, can once again walk amongst ruins that saw so much brutal action.

Continuing up the road, the next hairpin bend (the third) is close by Point 202 and the following bend marks Point 236, both sites were important to the battle. On the right, along the long straight that leads up from the fourth hairpin bend, can be seen Hangman's Hill, with its large rocky outcrop dominating the road, which passes round it in a series of sharp turns. This is Point 435 and the hill got its name from the remains of a pylon that stood on its top, appearing to the troops below like some gibbet on an English hill. It was on this knoll that the exposed contingent of Gurkhas held out for nine days, with the enemy in the Monastery above them.

Commonwealth War Cemetery beneath Montecassino on the edge of Cassino town near to the station area. The Liri valley is to the left and Monte Trocchio is to the rear. (Ken Ford)

General Mark Clark, Commander US Fifth Army, accompanied by MajGen Geoffrey Keyes, Commander US II Corps, proudly stand at the gates of Rome, the prize that Clark had striven so hard to make his own. (Imperial War Museum, TA26381)

All the way up the road magnificent views of the surrounding countryside can be obtained. Even those with a limited appreciation of military strategy cannot fail to recognise the tactical importance of this mountain feature. Its command of the terrain, the town below and Route 6 winding round the base of the hill is complete. At the top of the road up Montecassino we pass right beneath the high walls of the Monastery and it is from here that the holy building looks more like a fortress than ever. If we look away across to the right we can see the ground that succeeding Allied units toiled so fearlessly to cross. The terrain drops down steeply and then rises to the hills whose heights gave them their names. Points 444, 450 and 475 all mark the skyline. Rising above them all in the far distance is Monte Cairo. To the right, a few hundred yards away down a small road, is the Polish War Cemetery. It is sited beneath Snakeshead Ridge, with the rock face of Point 569 towering above it. Further along the ridge is the white column that marks the site of Point 593, for so long an elusive objective for the American, Indian and Polish troops.

Back down in the valley of the River Rapido, the crossing places of 34th Division north of the town are now criss-crossed by roads and buildings. A trip along the road to the village of Cairo will find the German War Cemetery. Opposite is the re-entrant through the hills up which all stores and ammunition destined for the troops on the peaks around Monastery Hill had to be carried. This was the only route to the beleaguered men in their exposed positions. Cavendish Road also started from this village.

On the other side of Cassino to the south, not too far from the Railway Station, is the Commonwealth War Cemetery. Further south along the Rapido on the wide opening to the Liri valley are the crossing places used in Operation Diadem and the fateful site near Sant' Angelo of the disaster suffered by Gen Walker's Texas Division. Sant' Angelo has been rebuilt and a memorial to the Americans stands by the bridge on the outskirts of the village. Even here the Monastery on Montecassino glowers down.

BIBLIOGRAPHY

Anders, Lt Gen W., *An Army in Exile* (London, 1949)

Blaxland, Gregory, *Alexander's Generals* (London, 1979)

Blumenson, Martin, *Salerno To Cassino* (Washington, 1969)

Ellis, John, *Cassino: The Hollow Victory* (London, 1984)

Ford, Ken, *Battleaxe Division* (Stroud, 1999)

Ford, Ken, *Cassino: The Four Battles*, (Marlborough, 2001)

Graham, Dominick & Bidwell, Shelford, *Tug of War: The Battle For Italy* (London, 1986)

Kesselring, Albrecht, *The Memoirs* (London, 1964)

Kuhn, Volkmar, *German Paratroopers in World War Two* (London, 1978)

Linklater, Eric, *The Campaign In Italy* (London, 1951)

Majdalany, Fred, *Cassino: Portrait of a Battle* (London, 1957)

Molony, Brig C.J.C., *The Mediterranean and Middle East Volume V* (London, 1973)

Senger und Etterlin, Fridolin von, *Neither Fear Nor Hope* (London, 1963)

Smith, E.C.D., *The Battles for Cassino* (Shepperton, 1975)

Stevens, G.R., *The Fourth Indian Division* (London, 1948)

INDEX

Figures in **bold** refer to illustrations

95